React Design Patterns and Best Practices

Build easy to scale modular applications using the most powerful components and design patterns

Michele Bertoli

BIRMINGHAM - MUMBAI

React Design Patterns and Best Practices

First published: January 2017

Production reference: 1100117

Published by Packt Publishing Ltd.
Livery Place
35 Livery Street
Birmingham
B32PB, UK.

ISBN 978-1-78646-453-8

www.packtpub.com

Credits

Author

Michele Bertoli

Reviewer

Clay Diffrient

Commissioning Editor

Ashwin Nair

Acquisition Editor

Shweta Pant

Content Development Editor

Onkar Wani

Technical Editor

Rashil Shah

Copy Editor

Safis Editing

Project Coordinator

Ulhas Kambali

Proofreader

Safis Editing

Indexer

Rekha Nair

Graphics

Abhinash Sahu

Production Coordinator

Aparna Bhagat

About the Author

Michele Bertoli is a frontend engineer with a passion for beautiful UIs. Born in Italy, he moved to London with his family to look for new and exciting job opportunities. He has a degree in computer science and loves clean and well-tested code. Currently, he is working with React.js, crafting modern JavaScript applications. He is a big fan of open source and is always trying to learn something new.

I would like to thank my wife and my son for making my days better with their smiles. Dante, I hope the time I spent writing the book instead of playing with you will make sense when you are older, and you will be proud of me. I would also like to thank Packt Publishing for giving me this opportunity.

About the Reviewer

Clay Diffrient is a JavaScript enthusiast who is always looking to improve and do more. He currently works mostly in React, but has proficiency with other frameworks and libraries, such as Angular, Backbone, and jQuery. He is a maintainer of the popular react-modal library. He takes joy in creating software that is accessible for all people.

Clay currently works as a software engineer at Instructure, where they make software that makes people smarter. He currently works on Instructure's flagship product, Canvas, an open source learning management system.

Clay has previously reviewed *MEAN Web Development* (ISBN: 9781783983285), and enjoys being involved with the community.

I wish to thank my wife Rachael and my two sons, Roger and Beau, for their unending support of my continual learning.

www.PacktPub.com

For support files and downloads related to your book, please visit www.PacktPub.com.

Did you know that Packt offers eBook versions of every book published, with PDF and ePub files available? You can upgrade to the eBook version at www.PacktPub.com and as a print book customer, you are entitled to a discount on the eBook copy. Get in touch with us at service@packtpub.com for more details.

At www.PacktPub.com, you can also read a collection of free technical articles, sign up for a range of free newsletters and receive exclusive discounts and offers on Packt books and eBooks.

https://www.packtpub.com/mapt

Get the most in-demand software skills with Mapt. Mapt gives you full access to all Packt books and video courses, as well as industry-leading tools to help you plan your personal development and advance your career.

Why subscribe?

- Fully searchable across every book published by Packt
- Copy and paste, print, and bookmark content
- On demand and accessible via a web browser

Customer Feedback

Thank you for purchasing this Packt book. We take our commitment to improving our content and products to meet your needs seriously--that's why your feedback is so valuable. Whatever your feelings about your purchase, please consider leaving a review on this book's Amazon page. Not only will this help us, more importantly it will also help others in the community to make an informed decision about the resources that they invest in to learn.

You can also review for us on a regular basis by joining our reviewers' club. **If you're interested in joining, or would like to learn more about the benefits we offer, please contact us**: customerreviews@packtpub.com.

Table of Contents

Preface

Taking a complete journey through the most valuable design patterns in React, this book demonstrates how to apply design patterns and best practices in real-life situations, whether it's for new or already existing projects. It will help you make your applications more flexible, perform better, and easier to maintain--giving your workflow a huge boost when it comes to speed, without reducing quality.

We'll begin by understanding the internals of React before gradually moving on to writing clean and maintainable code. We'll build components that are reusable across the application, structure applications, and create forms that actually work.

Then, we'll style React components and optimize them to make applications faster and more responsive. Finally, we'll write tests effectively, and you'll learn how to contribute to React and its ecosystem.

By the end of the book, you'll be saved from a lot of trial and error and developmental headaches, and you will be on the road to becoming a React expert.

What this book covers

Chapter 1, *Everything You Should Know About React*, introduces you to the base concepts of React, seen from an advanced perspective.

Chapter 2, *Clean Up Your Code*, teaches that one of the most important aspects of writing maintainable code is to keep it clean and follow a coding style guide. To use React, it is also important to know the basics of functional programming.

Chapter 3, *Create Truly Reusable Components*, informs that building an application using components is a key factor, but creating truly reusable components is the most important thing to do in order to keep the codebase clean and maintainable.

Chapter 4, *Compose All the Things*, says that real applications are created using different components and it's important to make them communicate effectively, organizing and structuring the hierarchy in the right way.

Chapter 5, *Proper Data Fetching*, instructs that any client-side application has to deal with data at some point; it takes you through the different techniques and approaches that can be used to fetch data in the React-way.

Chapter 6, *Write Code for the Browser*, states that our applications live in the browser and we should know how to use it properly. This chapter will go through some advanced concepts, such as events, animations, and how to interact with the DOM.

Chapter 7, *Make Your Components Look Beautiful*, demonstrates that crafting beautiful UI components is a big part of the frontend engineering work. With React, there are different ways of doing it and each one tackles the problem from a different perspective. It's important to know which libraries are available and how they work in order to choose the right one.

Chapter 8, *Server-Side Rendering for Fun and Profit*, instructs that one of the greatest features of React is the server-side rendering. It works out of the box, but it's important to learn how to use it in the right way to get the most out of it.

Chapter 9, *Improve the Performance of Your Applications*, informs that on the Web, performance is one of the most important factors to engage users. React offers a set of tools and techniques to create lightning-fast applications, and this chapter goes through all of them.

Chapter 10, *About Testing and Debugging*, makes you realize that we all want our applications to be stable and handle all the edge cases: tests help with that. Writing a comprehensive set of tests is vital to creating rock-solid and maintainable code. On the other hand, bugs always happen and it's crucial to know how to debug and find an issue as early as possible.

Chapter 11, *Anti-Patterns to Be Avoided*, explains the fact that developers often try to use shortcuts and creative solutions, but in some cases these workarounds can be dangerous for their applications, especially with big teams and large codebases. This chapter takes you through the common anti-patterns to be avoided while using React.

Chapter 12, *Next Steps*, is the last chapter, and all the topics have been covered. I believe it's important to mention how to open source components (to give back to the community) and how to contribute to React and its ecosystem.

What you need for this book

We will need a computer with a terminal, a node.js/npm environment, and a browser.

Who this book is for

If you want to increase your understanding of React and apply it to real-life application development, this book is for you.

Conventions

In this book, you will find a number of text styles that distinguish between different kinds of information. Here are some examples of these styles and an explanation of their meaning.

Code words in text, database table names, folder names, filenames, file extensions, pathnames, dummy URLs, user input, and Twitter handles are shown as follows: "Inside the loop, there is some conditional logic to check if the `#first` and the `#link` properties exist, and depending on their values, a different piece of HTML is rendered. Variables are wrapped into curly braces."

A block of code is set as follows:

```
const toLowerCase = input => {
  const output = []
  for (let i = 0; i < input.length; i++) {
    output.push(input[i].toLowerCase())
  }
  return output
}
```

Any command-line input or output is written as follows:

```
npm install -g create-react-app
```

New terms and **important words** are shown in bold. Words that you see on the screen, for example, in menus or dialog boxes, appear in the text like this: "Let's begin updating the tests, starting with the **renders with text** ones."

Warnings or important notes appear in a box like this.

 Tips and tricks appear like this.

Reader feedback

Feedback from our readers is always welcome. Let us know what you think about this book-what you liked or disliked. Reader feedback is important for us as it helps us develop titles that you will really get the most out of. To send us general feedback, simply e-mail feedback@packtpub.com, and mention the book's title in the subject of your message. If there is a topic that you have expertise in and you are interested in either writing or contributing to a book, see our author guide at www.packtpub.com/authors.

Customer support

Now that you are the proud owner of a Packt book, we have a number of things to help you to get the most from your purchase.

Downloading the example code

You can download the example code files for this book from your account at http://www.packtpub.com. If you purchased this book elsewhere, you can visit http://www.packtpub.com/support and register to have the files e-mailed directly to you.

You can download the code files by following these steps:

1. Log in or register to our website using your e-mail address and password.
2. Hover the mouse pointer on the **SUPPORT** tab at the top.
3. Click on **Code Downloads & Errata**.
4. Enter the name of the book in the **Search** box.
5. Select the book for which you're looking to download the code files.
6. Choose from the drop-down menu where you purchased this book from.
7. Click on **Code Download**.

Once the file is downloaded, please make sure that you unzip or extract the folder using the latest version of:

- WinRAR / 7-Zip for Windows
- Zipeg / iZip / UnRarX for Mac
- 7-Zip / PeaZip for Linux

The code bundle for the book is also hosted on GitHub at `https://github.com/PacktPubl ishing/React-Design-Patterns-and-Best-Practices`. We also have other code bundles from our rich catalog of books and videos available at `https://github.com/PacktPublish ing/`. Check them out!

Errata

Although we have taken every care to ensure the accuracy of our content, mistakes do happen. If you find a mistake in one of our books-maybe a mistake in the text or the code-we would be grateful if you could report this to us. By doing so, you can save other readers from frustration and help us improve subsequent versions of this book. If you find any errata, please report them by visiting `http://www.packtpub.com/submit-errata`, selecting your book, clicking on the **Errata Submission Form** link, and entering the details of your errata. Once your errata are verified, your submission will be accepted and the errata will be uploaded to our website or added to any list of existing errata under the Errata section of that title.

To view the previously submitted errata, go to `https://www.packtpub.com/books/conten t/support` and enter the name of the book in the search field. The required information will appear under the **Errata** section.

Piracy

Piracy of copyrighted material on the Internet is an ongoing problem across all media. At Packt, we take the protection of our copyright and licenses very seriously. If you come across any illegal copies of our works in any form on the Internet, please provide us with the location address or website name immediately so that we can pursue a remedy.

Please contact us at `copyright@packtpub.com` with a link to the suspected pirated material.

We appreciate your help in protecting our authors and our ability to bring you valuable content.

Questions

If you have a problem with any aspect of this book, you can contact us at questions@packtpub.com, and we will do our best to address the problem.

1
Everything You Should Know About React

Hello, readers!

This book assumes that you already know what React is and what problems it solves for you. You may have written a small/medium application with React and you want to improve your skills and answer all your open questions.

You should know that React is maintained by developers at Facebook and hundreds of contributors within the JavaScript community.

React is one of the most popular libraries for creating user interfaces and it is well-known to be fast, thanks to its smart way of touching the DOM.

It comes with JSX, a new syntax to write markup in JavaScript, which requires you to change your mind regarding the separation of concerns. It has many cool features, such as the server-side rendering that gives you the power to write Universal applications.

To follow this book, you will need to know how to use the terminal to install and run `npm` packages in your `Node.js` environment.

All the examples are written in ES2015, which you should be able to read and understand.

In this first chapter, we will go through some basics concepts which are important to master to use React effectively, but are non-trivial to figure out for beginners:

- The difference between imperative and declarative programming
- React components and their instances, and how React uses elements to control the UI flow

- How React changes the way we build web applications, enforcing a different new concept of separation of concerns, and the reasons behind its unpopular design choice
- Why people feel the JavaScript Fatigue and what you can do to avoid the most common errors developers make when approaching the React ecosystem

Declarative programming

Reading the React documentation or blog posts about React, you have surely come across the term **declarative**.

In fact, one of the reasons why React is so powerful is because it enforces a declarative programming paradigm.

Consequently, to master React, it is important to understand what declarative programming means and what the main differences between imperative and declarative programming are.

The easiest way to approach the problem is to think about imperative programming as a way of describing how things work, and declarative programming as a way of describing what you want to achieve.

A real-life parallel in the imperative world would be entering a bar for a beer, and giving the following instructions to the bartender:

- Take a glass from the shelf
- Put the glass in front of the draft
- Pull down the handle until the glass is full
- Pass me the glass

In the declarative world, instead, you would just say: "Beer, please."

The declarative approach of asking for a beer assumes that the bartender knows how to serve one, and that is an important aspect of the way declarative programming works.

Let's move into a JavaScript example, writing a simple function that, given an array of uppercase strings, returns an array with the same strings in lowercase:

```
toLowerCase(['FOO', 'BAR']) // ['foo', 'bar']
```

An imperative function to solve the problem would be implemented as follows:

```
const toLowerCase = input => {
  const output = []
  for (let i = 0; i < input.length; i++) {
    output.push(input[i].toLowerCase())
  }
  return output
}
```

First of all, an empty array to contain the result gets created. Then, the function loops through all the elements of the input array and pushes the lowercase values into the empty array. Finally, the output array gets returned.

A declarative solution would be as follows:

```
const toLowerCase = input => input.map(
  value => value.toLowerCase()
)
```

The items of the input array are passed to a map function, which returns a new array containing the lowercase values.

There are some important differences to note: the former example is less elegant and it requires more effort to be understood. The latter is terser and easier to read, which makes a huge difference in big code bases, where maintainability is crucial.

Another aspect worth mentioning is that in the declarative example, there is no need to use variables nor to keep their values updated during the execution. Declarative programming, in fact, tends to avoid creating and mutating a state.

As a final example, let's see what it means for React to be declarative.

The problem we will try to solve is a common task in web development: showing a map with a marker.

The JavaScript implementation (using the Google Maps SDK) is as follows:

```
const map = new google.maps.Map(document.getElementById('map'), {
  zoom: 4,
  center: myLatLng,
})

const marker = new google.maps.Marker({
  position: myLatLng,
  title: 'Hello World!',
})
```

[9]

```
marker.setMap(map)
```

It is clearly imperative, because all the instructions needed to create the map, and create the marker and attach it to the map are described inside the code, one after the other.

A React component to show a map on a page would look like this instead:

```
<Gmaps zoom={4} center={myLatLng}>
  <Marker position={myLatLng} Hello world! />
</Gmaps>
```

In declarative programming, developers only describe what they want to achieve and there's no need to list all the steps to make it work.

The fact that React offers a declarative approach makes it easy to use, and consequently, the resulting code is simple, which often leads to fewer bugs and more maintainability.

React elements

This book assumes that you are familiar with components and their instances, but there is another object you should know if you want to use React effectively: the **Element**.

Whenever you call `createClass`, extend `Component`, or simply declare a stateless function, you are creating a component. React manages all the instances of your components at runtime, and there can be more than one instance of the same component in memory at a given point in time.

As mentioned previously, React follows a declarative paradigm, and there's no need to tell it how to interact with the DOM; you just declare what you want to see on the screen and React does the job for you.

As you might have already experienced, most other UI libraries work in the opposite way: they leave the responsibility of keeping the interface updated to the developer, who has to manage the creation and destruction of the DOM elements manually.

To control the UI flow, React uses a particular type of object, called **element**, which describes what has to be shown on the screen. These immutable objects are much simpler compared to the components and their instances, and contain only the information that is strictly needed to represent the interface.

The following is an example of an element:

```
{
  type: Title,
  props: {
    color: 'red',
    children: 'Hello, Title!'
  }
}
```

Elements have a type, which is the most important attribute, and some properties. There is also a special property, called **children**, which is optional and represents the direct descendant of the element.

The type is important because it tells React how to deal with the element itself. In fact, if the type is a string, the element represents a **DOM node**, while if the type is a function, the element is a **component**.

DOM elements and components can be nested with each other, to represent the render tree:

```
{
  type: Title,
  props: {
    color: 'red',
    children: {
      type: 'h1',
      props: {
        children: 'Hello, H1!'
      }
    }
  }
}
```

When the type of the element is a function, React calls it, passing the props to get back the underlying elements. It keeps on performing the same operation recursively on the result until it gets a tree of DOM nodes, which React can render on the screen. This process is called **reconciliation**, and it is used by both React DOM and React Native to create the user interfaces of their respective platforms.

Unlearning everything

Using React for the first time usually requires an open mind because it brings a new way of designing web and mobile applications. In fact, React tries to innovate the way we build user interfaces following a path that breaks most of the well-known best practices.

In the last two decades, we learned that the separation of concerns is important, and we used to think about it in terms of separating the logic from the templates. Our goal has always been to write the JavaScript and the HTML in different files.

Various templating solutions have been created to help developers achieve this.

The problem is that most of the time, that kind of separation is just an illusion and the truth is that the JavaScript and the HTML are tightly coupled, no matter where they live.

Let's see an example of a template:

```
{{#items}}
  {{#first}}
    <li><strong>{{name}}</strong></li>
  {{/first}}
  {{#link}}
    <li><a href="{{url}}">{{name}}</a></li>
  {{/link}}
{{/items}}
```

The preceding snippet is taken from the website of **Mustache**, one of the most popular templating systems.

The first row tells Mustache to loop through a collection of items. Inside the loop, there is some conditional logic to check if the #first and the #link properties exist, and depending on their values, a different piece of HTML is rendered. Variables are wrapped into curly braces.

If your application has only to display some variables, a templating library could represent a good solution, but when it comes to starting to work with complex data structures, things change.

In fact, templating systems and their Domain-Specific Language (DSL) offer a subset of features, and they try to provide the functionalities of a real programming language without reaching the same level of completeness.

As shown in the example, templates highly depend on the models they receive from the logic layer to display the information.

On the other hand, JavaScript interacts with the DOM elements rendered by the templates to update the UI, even if they are loaded from separate files.

The same problem applies to styles: they are defined in a different file, but they are referenced in the templates and the CSS selectors follow the structure of the markup, so it is almost impossible to change one without breaking the other, which is the definition of coupling.

That is why the classic separation of concerns ended up being more a separation of technologies, which is of course not a bad thing, but it does not solve any real problems.

React tries to move a step forward by putting the templates where they belong: next to the logic. The reason it does that is because React suggests you organize your applications by composing small bricks called **components**.

The framework should not tell you how to separate the concerns, because every application has its own, and only the developers should decide how to limit the boundaries of their apps.

The component-based approach drastically changes the way we write web applications, which is why the classic concept of separation of concerns is gradually being taken over by a much more modern structure.

The paradigm enforced by React is not new, and it was not invented by its creators, but React has contributed to making the concept mainstream and, most importantly, popularized it in such a way that is easier to understand for developers with different levels of expertise.

This is how the render method of a React component looks:

```
render() {
  return (
    <button style={{ color: 'red' }} onClick={this.handleClick}>
      Click me!
    </button>
  )
}
```

We all agree that it looks a bit weird in the beginning, but it is just because we are not used to that kind of syntax.

As soon as we learn it and we realize how powerful it is, we understand its potential.

Using JavaScript for both logic and templating not only helps us separate our concerns in a better way, but it also gives us more power and more expressivity, which is what we need to build complex user interfaces.

That is why, even if the idea of mixing JavaScript and HTML sounds weird in the beginning, it is important to give React five minutes.

The best way to get started with a new technology is to try it in a small side project and see how it goes. In general, the right approach is to always be ready to unlearn everything and change your mindset if the long-term benefits are worth it.

There is another concept, which is pretty controversial and hard to accept, and which the engineers behind React are trying to push to the community: moving the styling logic inside the component, too.

The end goal is to encapsulate every single technology used to create our components and separate the concerns according to their domain and functionalities.

Here is an example of a style object taken from the React documentation:

```
var divStyle = {
  color: 'white',
  backgroundImage: 'url(' + imgUrl + ')',
  WebkitTransition: 'all', // note the capital 'W' here
  msTransition: 'all' // 'ms' is the only lowercase vendor prefix
};

ReactDOM.render(
 <div style={divStyle}>Hello World!</div>,
 mountNode
);
```

This set of solutions, where developers use JavaScript to write their styles, is known as #CSSinJS, and we will talk about it extensively in Chapter 7, *Make Your Components Look Beautiful*.

Common misconceptions

There is a common opinion that React is a huge set of technologies and tools, and if you want to use it, you are forced to deal with package managers, transpilers, module bundlers, and an infinite list of different libraries.

This idea is so widespread and shared among people that it has been clearly defined, and has been given the name **JavaScript Fatigue**.

It is not hard to understand the reasons behind this. In fact, all the repositories and libraries in the React ecosystem are made using the shiny new technologies, the latest version of JavaScript, and the most advanced techniques and paradigms.

Moreover, there is a massive number of React boilerplates on GitHub, each one with tens of dependencies to offer solutions for any problems.

It is very easy to think that all these tools are required to start using React, but this is far from the truth.

Despite this common way of thinking, React is a pretty tiny library, and it can be used inside any page (or even inside a JSFiddle) in the same way everyone used to use jQuery or Backbone: just by including the script on the page before the closing body element.

To be fair, there are two scripts because React is split into two packages: `react`, which implements the core features of the library, and `react-dom`, which contains all the browser-related features. The reason behind that is because the core package is used to support different targets, such as React DOM in browsers and React Native on mobile devices.

Running a React application inside a single HTML page does not require any package manager or complex operation. You can just download the distribution bundle and host it yourself (or use `unpkg.com`), and you are ready to get started with React and its features in a few minutes.

Here are the URLs to be included in the HTML to start using React:

- `https://unpkg.com/react/dist/react.min.js`
- `https://unpkg.com/react-dom/dist/react-dom.min.js`

If we include the core React library only, we cannot use JSX because it is not a standard language supported by the browser; but, the whole point is to start with the bare minimum set of features and add more functionalities as soon as they are needed.

For a simple UI, we could just use `createElement` and, only when we start building something more complex, we can include a transpiler to enable JSX and convert it into JavaScript.

As soon as the app grows a bit more, we may need a router to handle different pages and views, and we can include that as well.

At some point, we may want to load data from some API endpoints, and if the application keeps growing, we will reach the point where we need some external dependencies to abstract complex operations. Only in that very moment, should we introduce a package manager.

Then the time will come to split our application into separate modules and organize our files in the right way. At that point, we should start thinking about using a module bundler.

Following this very simple approach, there's no fatigue.

Starting with a boilerplate that has one hundred dependencies and tens of npm packages of which we know nothing is the best way to get lost.

It is important to note that every programming-related job (and front end engineering in particular) requires continuous learning. It is the nature of the Web to evolve at a very fast pace and change according to the needs of both users and developers. This is the way our environment has worked since the beginning and what makes it very exciting.

As we gain experience working on the Web, we learn that we cannot master everything and we should find the right way to keep ourselves updated to avoid the fatigue. We become able to follow all the new trends without jumping into the new libraries for the sake of it, unless we have time for a side project.

It is astonishing how, in the JavaScript world, as soon as a specification is announced or drafted, someone in the community implements it as a transpiler plugin or a polyfill, letting everyone else play with it while the browser vendors agree and start supporting it.

This is something that makes JavaScript and the browser a completely different environment compared to any other language or platform.

The downside of it is that things change very quickly, but it is just a matter of finding the right balance between betting on new technologies versus staying safe.

In any case, Facebook developers care a lot about the DX (developer experience), and they listen carefully to the community. So, even if it is not true that to use React we are required to learn hundreds of different tools, they realized that people were feeling the fatigue and they released a CLI tool that makes it incredibly easy to scaffold and run a real React application.

The only requirement is to use a node.js/npm environment and install the CLI tool globally:

```
npm install -g create-react-app
```

When the executable is installed, we can use it to create our application passing a folder name:

```
create-react-app hello-world
```

Finally, we move into the folder of our application with cd hello-world and we just run:

```
npm start
```

Magically, our application is running with a single dependency, but with all the features needed to build a complete React application using the most advanced techniques. The following screenshot shows the default page of an application created with create-react-app:

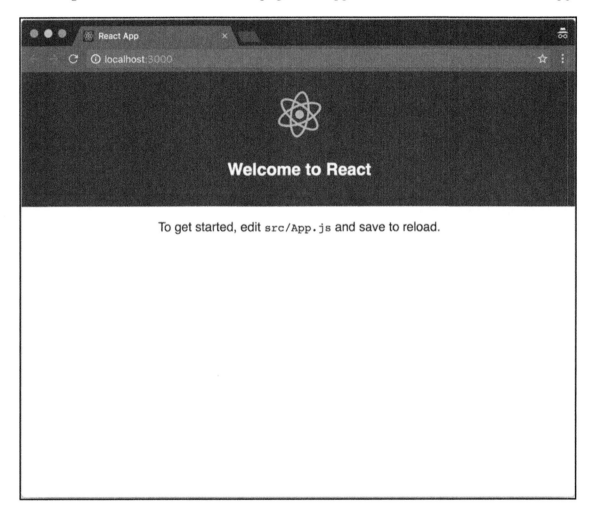

We will use this tool throughout the book to run the examples for each chapter which are also available on GitHub at the following address:

https://github.com/MicheleBertoli/react-design-patterns-and-best-practices

Summary

In this first chapter, we have learned some basic concepts that are very important for following the rest of the book, and which are crucial to working with React daily.

We now know how to write declarative code and we have a clear understanding of the difference between the components we create and the elements React uses to display their instances on the screen.

We learned the reasons behind the choice of co-locating logic and templates together, and why that unpopular decision has been a big win for React.

We went through the reasons why it is common to feel fatigue in the JavaScript ecosystem, but we have also seen how to avoid those problems by following an iterative approach.

Finally, we have seen what the new `create-react-app` CLI is, and we are now ready to start writing some real code.

2
Clean Up Your Code

This chapter assumes that you already have experience with JSX and you want to improve your skills to use it effectively.

To use JSX without any problems or unexpected behaviors, it is important to understand how it works under the hood and the reasons why it is a useful tool for building UIs.

Our goal is to write clean and maintainable JSX code, and to achieve that, we have to know where it comes from, how it gets translated to JavaScript, and which features it provides.

In the first section, we will do a little step back, but please bear with me because it is crucial to master the basics in order to apply the best practices.

In this chapter, we will cover the following topics:

- What JSX is and why we should use it
- What Babel is and how we can use it to write modern JavaScript code
- The main features of JSX and the differences between HTML and JSX
- Best practices to write JSX in an elegant and maintainable way
- How linting, and ESLint in particular, can make our JavaScript code consistent across applications and teams
- The basics of functional programming and why following a functional paradigm will make us write better React components

JSX

In the previous chapter, we saw how React changes the concept of separation of concerns, moving the boundaries inside components.

We also learned how React uses the elements returned by the components to display the UI on the screen.

Let's now see how we can declare our elements inside our components.

React provides two ways to define our elements. The first one is by using JavaScript functions, and the second one is by using JSX, an optional XML-like syntax. Here is the examples section of the official React.js website:

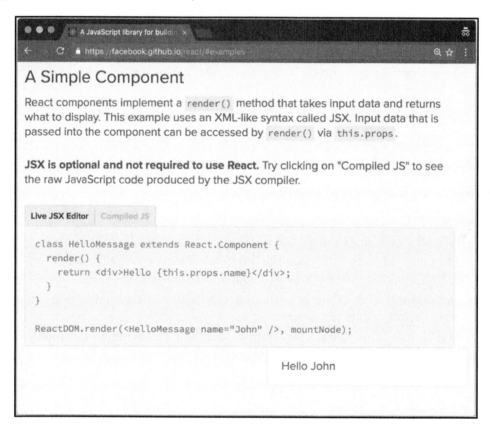

To begin with, JSX is one of the main reasons why people fail to approach React, because looking at the examples on the home page and seeing JavaScript mixed with HTML for the first time seems strange to most of us.

As soon as we get used to it, we realize that it is very convenient, precisely because it is similar to HTML and looks very familiar to anyone who has already created UIs on the web.

The opening and closing tags make it easier to represent nested trees of elements–something that would have been unreadable and hard to maintain using plain JavaScript.

Babel

In order to use JSX (and some features of ES2015) in our code, we have to install **Babel**.

First of all, it is important to clearly understand the problems it can solve for us and why we need to add a step to our process. The reason is that we want to use features of the language that have not yet been added in the browser, our target environment. Those advanced features make our code cleaner for developers, but the browser cannot understand and execute it.

The solution is to write our scripts in JSX and ES2015, and when we are ready to ship, we compile the sources into ES5, the standard specification implemented in major browsers today.

 Babel is a popular JavaScript compiler widely adopted within the React community.

Babel can compile ES2015 code into ES5 JavaScript, as well as compile JSX into JavaScript functions. The process is called transpilation, because it compiles the source into a new source rather than into an executable.

Using it is pretty straightforward; we just install it:

```
npm install --global babel-cli
```

If you do not want to install it globally (developers usually tend to avoid this), you can install Babel locally to a project and run it through an npm script, but for the purposes of this chapter, a global instance is fine.

When the installation is complete, we can run the following command to compile any JavaScript file:

```
babel source.js -o output.js
```

One of the reasons Babel is so powerful is because it is highly configurable. Babel is just a tool to transpile a source file into an output file, but to apply some transformations, we need to configure it.

Luckily, there are some very useful presets of configurations, which we can easily install and use:

```
npm install --global babel-preset-es2015
babel-preset-react
```

Once the installation is complete, we create a configuration file called .babelrc in the root folder, and put the following lines into it to tell Babel to use those presets:

```
{
  "presets": [
    "es2015",
    "react"
  ]
}
```

From this point on, we can write ES2015 and JSX in our source files and execute the output files in the browser.

Hello, World!

Now that our environment has been set up to support JSX, we can dive into the most basic example: generating a div element.

This is how you would create a div with React's createElement function:

```
React.createElement('div')
```

And this is the JSX for creating a `div` element:

```
<div />
```

It looks similar to regular HTML.

The big difference is that we are writing the markup inside a `.js` file, but it is important to note that JSX is only syntactic sugar and it gets transpiled into JavaScript before being executed in the browser.

In fact, our `<div />` is translated into `React.createElement('div')` when we run Babel, which is something we should always keep in mind when we write our templates.

DOM elements and React components

With JSX, we can create both HTML elements and React components; the only difference is whether or not they start with a capital letter.

For example, to render an HTML button, we use `<button />`, while to render our `Button` components we use `<Button />`.

The first button is transpiled into the following:

```
React.createElement('button')
```

The second one is transpiled into the following:

```
React.createElement(Button)
```

The difference here is that in the first call we are passing the type of the DOM element as a string, while in the second call we are passing the component itself, which means that it should exist in the scope to work.

As you may have noticed, JSX supports self-closing tags, which are pretty good for keeping the code terse and do not require us to repeat unnecessary tags.

Props

JSX is very convenient when your DOM elements or React components have props. In fact, using XML is pretty easy to set attributes on elements:

```
<imgsrc="https://facebook.github.io/react/img/logo.svg"
alt="React.js" />
```

The equivalent in JavaScript would be as follows:

```
React.createElement("img", {
  src: "https://facebook.github.io/react/img/logo.svg",
  alt: "React.js"
});
```

This is far less readable, and even with only a couple of attributes it is harder to read without a bit of reasoning.

Children

JSX allows you to define children to describe the tree of elements and compose complex UIs.

A basic example is a link with text inside it, as follows:

```
<a href="https://facebook.github.io/react/">Click me!</a>
```

This would be transpiled into the following:

```
React.createElement(
  "a",
  { href: "https://facebook.github.io/react/" },
  "Click me!"
);
```

Our link can be enclosed inside a `div` for some layout requirements, and the JSX snippet to achieve that is as follows:

```
<div>
  <a href="https://facebook.github.io/react/">Click me!</a>
</div>
```

The JavaScript equivalent is as follows:

```
React.createElement(
  "div",
  null,
  React.createElement(
    "a",
    { href: "https://facebook.github.io/react/" },
    "Click me!"
  )
);
```

It should now be clear how the XML-like syntax of JSX makes everything more readable and maintainable, but it is always important to know the JavaScript parallel of our JSX in order to have control over the creation of elements.

The good part is that we are not limited to having elements as children of elements, but we can use JavaScript expressions such as functions or variables.

To do this, we just have to enclose expression within curly braces:

```
<div>
  Hello, {variable}.
  I'm a {function()}.
</div>
```

The same applies to non-string attributes:

```
<a href={this.makeHref()}>Click me!</a>
```

Differences with HTML

So far, we have looked at the similarities between JSX and HTML. Let's now look at the little differences between them and the reasons they exist.

Attributes

We must always keep in mind that JSX is not a standard language and that it gets transpiled into JavaScript. Because of this, some attributes cannot be used.

For example, instead of `class`, we have to use `className`, and instead of `for`, we have to use `htmlFor`:

```
<label className="awesome-label" htmlFor="name" />
```

The reason for this is that `class` and `for` are reserved words in JavaScript.

Style

A pretty significant difference is the way the style attribute works. We will look at how to use it in more detail in `Chapter 7`, *Make Your Components Look Beautiful*, but now we will focus on the way it works.

The style attribute does not accept a CSS string as the HTML parallel does, but it expects a JS object where the style names are **camelCased**:

```
<div style={{ backgroundColor: 'red' }} />
```

Root

One important difference with HTML worth mentioning is that since JSX elements get translated into JavaScript functions and you cannot return two functions in JavaScript, whenever you have multiple elements at the same level, you are forced to wrap them into a parent.

Let's look at a simple example:

```
<div />
<div />
```

This gives us the following error:

```
Adjacent JSX elements must be wrapped in an enclosing tag
```

On the other hand, the following works:

```
<div>
  <div />
  <div />
</div>
```

It is pretty annoying to have to add unnecessary `div` tags just to make JSX work, but React developers are trying to find a solution (at the time of writing):

```
https://github.com/reactjs/core-notes/blob/master/2016-07/july-07.md
```

Spaces

There's one thing that could be a little bit tricky in the beginning, and again it concerns the fact that we should always keep in mind that JSX is not HTML, even if it has an XML-like syntax.

JSX, in fact, handles the spaces between text and elements differently from HTML, in a way that's counter-intuitive.

Consider the following snippet:

```
<div>
  <span>foo</span>
  bar
  <span>baz</span>
</div>
```

In the browser, which interprets HTML, this code would give you `foo bar baz`, which is exactly what we expect.

In JSX, instead, the same code would be rendered as `foobarbaz`, which is because the three nested lines get transpiled as individual children of the `div` element, without taking the spaces into account. A common solution to get the same output, is putting a space explicitly between the elements:

```
<div>
  <span>foo</span>
  {' '}
  bar
  {' '}
  <span>baz</span>
</div>
```

As you may have noticed, we are using an empty string wrapped inside a JavaScript expression to force the compiler to apply the space between the elements.

Boolean attributes

A couple more things worth mentioning before starting for real regarding the way you define Boolean attributes in JSX. If you set an attribute without a value, JSX assumes that its value is true, following the same behavior of the HTML `disabled` attribute, for example.

This means that if we want to set an attribute to false, we have to declare it explicitly as false:

```
<button disabled />
React.createElement("button", { disabled: true });
```

The following is another example:

```
<button disabled={false} />
React.createElement("button", { disabled: false });
```

This can be confusing in the beginning because we may think that omitting an attribute would mean false, but it is not like that. With React, we should always be explicit to avoid confusion.

Spread attributes

An important feature is the **spread attributes** operator, which comes from the Rest/Spread Properties for ECMAScript proposal, (`https://github.com/sebmarkbage/ecmascript-rest-spread`) and is very convenient whenever we want to pass all the attributes of a JavaScript object to an element.

A common practice that leads to fewer bugs is not to pass entire JavaScript objects down to children by reference, but to use their primitive values, which can be easily validated, making components more robust and error-proof.

Let's see how it works:

```
const foo = { id: 'bar' }
return <div {...foo} />
```

The preceding code gets transpiled into the following:

```
var foo = { id: 'bar' };
return React.createElement('div', foo);
```

JavaScript templating

Finally, we started with the assumption that one of the advantages of moving the templates inside our components instead of using an external template library is that we can use the full power of JavaScript, so let's start looking at what that means.

The spread attributes is an example of that, and another common example is that JavaScript expressions can be used as attributes values by enclosing them within curly braces:

```
<button disabled={errors.length} />
```

Common patterns

Now that we know how JSX works and can master it, we are ready to see how to use it in the right way following some useful conventions and techniques.

Multi-line

Let's start with a very simple one. As stated previously, one of the main reasons we should prefer JSX over React's `createElement` is because of its XML-like syntax and because balanced opening and closing tags are perfect to represent a tree of nodes.

Therefore, we should try to use it in the right way and get the most out of it.

One example is as follows; whenever we have nested elements, we should always go multiline:

```
<div>
  <Header />
  <div>
    <Main content={...} />
  </div>
</div>
```

This is preferable to the following:

```
<div><Header /><div><Main content={...} /></div></div>
```

The exception is if the children are not elements, such as text or variables. In that case, it makes sense to remain on the same line and avoid adding noise to the markup, as follows:

```
<div>
  <Alert>{message}</Alert>
  <Button>Close</Button>
</div>
```

Always remember to wrap your elements inside parentheses when you write them in multiple lines. In fact, JSX always gets replaced by functions, and functions written on a new line can give you an unexpected result because of automatic semicolon insertion. Suppose, for example, you are returning JSX from your render method, which is how you create UIs in React.

The following example works fine, because the `div` is on the same line as the return:

```
return <div />
```

The following, however, is not right:

```
return
  <div />
```

The reason for this is because you would have the following:

```
return;
React.createElement("div", null);
```

This is why you have to wrap the statement in parentheses:

```
return (
  <div />
)
```

Multi-properties

A common problem in writing JSX comes when an element has multiples attributes. One solution is to write all the attributes on the same line, but this would lead to very long lines, which we do not want in our code (see the following section for how to enforce coding style guides).

A common solution is to write each attribute on a new line, with one level of indentation, and then align the closing bracket with the opening tag:

```
<button
  foo="bar"
  veryLongPropertyName="baz"
  onSomething={this.handleSomething}
/>
```

Conditionals

Things get more interesting when we start working with **conditionals**, for example, if we want to render some components only when certain conditions are matched. The fact that we can use JavaScript in our conditions is a big plus, but there are many different ways to express conditions in JSX and it is important to understand the benefits and problems of each one of these in order to write code that is both readable and maintainable.

Suppose we want to show a logout button only if the user is currently logged into our application.

A simple snippet to start with is as follows:

```
let button
if (isLoggedIn) {
  button = <LogoutButton />
}
return <div>{button}</div>
```

This works, but it is not very readable, especially if there are multiple components and multiple conditions.

In JSX, we can use an inline condition:

```
<div>
  {isLoggedIn && <LoginButton />}
</div>
```

This works because if the condition is false, nothing gets rendered, but if the condition is true, the `createElement` function of the `LoginButton` gets called and the element is returned to compose the resulting tree.

If the condition has an alternative, (the classic `if...else` statement), and we want, for example, to show a logout button if the user is logged in and a login button otherwise, we can use JavaScript's `if...else`, as follows:

```
let button
if (isLoggedIn) {
  button = <LogoutButton />
} else {
  button = <LoginButton />
}
return <div>{button}</div>
```

Alternatively, and better, we can use a ternary condition, which makes the code more compact:

```
<div>
  {isLoggedIn ? <LogoutButton /> : <LoginButton />}
</div>
```

You can find the ternary condition used in popular repositories such as the Redux realworld example (`https://github.com/reactjs/redux/blob/master/examples/real-world/src/components/List.js#L25`), where the ternary is used to show a loading label if the component is fetching the data, or *load more* inside a button depending on the value of the `isFetching` variable:

```
<button [...]>
```

```
    {isFetching ? 'Loading...' : 'Load More'}
  </button>
```

Let's now look at the best solution for when things get more complicated and, for example, we have to check more than one variable to determine whether to render a component or not:

```
<div>
  {dataIsReady && (isAdmin || userHasPermissions) &&
    <SecretData />
  }
</div>
```

In this case, it is clear that using the inline condition is a good solution, but the readability is strongly impacted. Instead, we can create a helper function inside our component and use it in JSX to verify the condition:

```
canShowSecretData() {
  const { dataIsReady, isAdmin, userHasPermissions } = this.props
  return dataIsReady && (isAdmin || userHasPermissions)
}

<div>
  {this.canShowSecretData() && <SecretData />}
</div>
```

As you can see, this change makes the code more readable and the condition more explicit. If you look at this code in six months' time, you will still find it clear just by reading the name of the function.

If you do not like using functions, you can use an object's getters, which make the code more elegant.

For example, instead of declaring a function, we define a getter:

```
get canShowSecretData() {
  const { dataIsReady, isAdmin, userHasPermissions } = this.props
  return dataIsReady && (isAdmin || userHasPermissions)
}

<div>
  {this.canShowSecretData && <SecretData />}
</div>
```

The same applies to computed properties. Suppose you have two single properties, for currency and value. Instead of creating the price string inside your render method, you can create a class function:

```
getPrice() {
  return `${this.props.currency}${this.props.value}`
}

<div>{this.getPrice()}</div>
```

This is better, because it is isolated and you can easily test it in case it contains logic.

Alternatively, you can go a step further and, as we have just seen, use getters:

```
get price() {
  return `${this.props.currency}${this.props.value}`
}

<div>{this.price}</div>
```

Going back to conditional statements, there are other solutions that require using external dependencies. A good practice is to avoid external dependencies as much as we can to keep our bundle smaller, but it may be worth it in this particular case because improving the readability of our templates is a big win.

The first solution is `render-if`, which we can install with the following:

npm install --save render-if

We can then easily use it in our projects, as follows:

```
const { dataIsReady, isAdmin, userHasPermissions } = this.props
const canShowSecretData = renderIf(
  dataIsReady && (isAdmin || userHasPermissions)
)

<div>
  {canShowSecretData(<SecretData />)}
</div>
```

We wrap our conditions inside the `renderIf` function.

The utility function that gets returned can be used as a function, which receives the JSX markup to be shown when the condition is true.

One goal we should always keep in mind is to never add too much logic inside our components. Some of them will require a bit of it, but we should try to keep them as simple and dumb as possible so that we can easily spot and fix errors.

We should at least try to keep the `renderIf` method as clean as possible, and to do that, we can use another utility library called `react-only-if`, which lets us write our components as if the condition is always true by setting the conditional function using a Higher-Order Component.

We will talk about Higher-Order Components extensively in Chapter 4, *Compose All the Things*, but for now you just need to know that they are functions that receive a component and return an enhanced one by adding some properties or modifying its behavior.

To use the library, we just need to install it as follows:

```
npm install --save react-only-if
```

Once it is installed, we can use it in our apps in the following way:

```
const SecretDataOnlyIf = onlyIf(
  ({ dataIsReady, isAdmin, userHasPermissions }) => {
    return dataIsReady && (isAdmin || userHasPermissions)
  }
)(SecretData)

<div>
  <SecretDataOnlyIf
    dataIsReady={...}
    isAdmin={...}
    userHasPermissions={...}
  />
</div>
```

As you can see here, there is no logic at all inside the component itself.

We pass the condition as the first parameter of the `onlyIf` function and when the condition is matched, the component is rendered.

The function used to validate the condition receives the props, state, and context of the component.

In this way, we avoid polluting our component with conditionals so that it is easier to understand and reason about.

Loops

A very common operation in UI development is to display lists of items. When it comes to showing lists, using JavaScript as a template language is a very good idea.

If we write a function that returns an array inside our JSX template, each element of the array gets compiled into an element.

As we have seen before, we can use any JavaScript expressions inside curly braces and the most common way to generate an array of elements, given an array of objects, is to use map.

Let's dive into a real-world example. Suppose you have a list of users, each one with a name property attached to it.

To create an unordered list to show the users, you can do the following:

```
<ul>
  {users.map(user =><li>{user.name}</li>)}
</ul>
```

This snippet is incredibly simple and incredibly powerful at the same time, where the power of the HTML and JavaScript converge.

Control statements

Conditionals and loops are very common operations in UI templates and you may feel wrong using the JavaScript ternary or the map function to perform them. JSX has been built in such a way that it only abstracts the creation of the elements, leaving the logic parts to real JavaScript, which is great except that sometimes, the code becomes less clear.

In general, we aim to remove all the logic from our components, and especially from our render methods, but sometimes we have to show and hide elements according to the state of the application, and very often we have to loop through collections and arrays.

If you feel that using JSX for that kind of operation will make your code more readable, there is a Babel plugin available to do just that: jsx-control-statements.

This follows the same philosophy as JSX, and it does not add any real functionality to the language; it is just syntactic sugar that gets compiled into JavaScript.

Let's see how it works.

First of all, we have to install it:

```
npm install --save jsx-control-statements
```

Once it is installed, we have to add it to the list of our babel plugins in our `.babelrc` file:

```
"plugins": ["jsx-control-statements"]
```

From now on we can use the syntax provided by the plugin and Babel will transpile it together with the common JSX syntax.

A conditional statement written using the plugin looks like the following snippet:

```
<If condition={this.canShowSecretData}>
  <SecretData />
</If>
```

This gets transpiled into a ternary expression as follows:

```
{canShowSecretData ? <SecretData /> : null}
```

The `If` component is great, but if for some reason you have nested conditions in your render method, it can easily become messy and hard to follow. Here is where the `Choose` component comes in handy:

```
<Choose>
  <When condition={...}>
    <span>if</span>
  </When>
  <When condition={...}>
    <span>else if</span>
  </When>
  <Otherwise>
    <span>else</span>
  </Otherwise>
</Choose>
```

Please note that the preceding code gets transpiled into multiple ternaries.

Finally, there is a *component* (always remember that we are not talking about real components but just syntactic sugar) to manage the loops which is also very convenient:

```
<ul>
  <For each="user" of={this.props.users}>
    <li>{user.name}</li>
  </For>
</ul>
```

The preceding code gets transpiled into a map function–no magic there.

If you are used to using **linters**, you might wonder why the linter is not complaining about that code. In fact, the variable `user` does not exist before the transpilation, nor is it wrapped into a function. To avoid those linting errors, there is another plugin to install: `eslint-plugin-jsx-control-statements`.

If you did not understand the previous sentence, don't worry; we will talk about linting in the following section.

Sub-rendering

It is worth stressing that we always want to keep our components very small and our render methods very clean and simple.

However, that is not an easy goal, especially when you are creating an application iteratively and in the first iteration you are not sure exactly how to split the components into smaller ones.

So, what should we be doing when the render method becomes too big to maintain? One solution is to split it into smaller functions in a way that lets us keep all the logic in the same component.

Let's look at an example:

```
renderUserMenu() {
  // JSX for user menu
}

renderAdminMenu() {
  // JSX for admin menu
}

render() {
  return (
    <div>
      <h1>Welcome back!</h1>
      {this.userExists && this.renderUserMenu()}
      {this.userIsAdmin && this.renderAdminMenu()}
    </div>
  )
}
```

This is not always considered a best practice because it seems more obvious to split the component into smaller ones. However, sometimes it helps just to keep the render method cleaner. For example, in the Redux realworld examples, a sub-render method is used to render the load more button.

Now that we are JSX power users, it is time to move on and see how to follow a style guide within our code to make it consistent.

ESLint

We always try to write the best code possible, but sometimes errors happen, and spending a few hours catching a bug due to a typo is very frustrating. Luckily, there are some tools that can help us check the correctness of our code as soon as we type it.

These tools are not able to tell us if our code is going to do what it supposed to do, but they can help us to avoid syntactical errors.

If you come from a static language such as C#, you are used to getting that kind of warning inside your IDE.

Douglas Crockford made linting popular in JavaScript with JSLint (initially released in 2002) a few years ago; then we had JSHint and finally, the de-facto standard in the React world nowadays is *ESLint*.

ESLint is an open-source project released in 2013 that became popular thanks to the fact that it is highly configurable and extensible.

In the JavaScript ecosystem, where libraries and techniques change very quickly, it is crucial to have a tool that can be easily extended with plugins, and rules that can be enabled and disabled when needed.

Most importantly, nowadays we use transpilers such as Babel, and experimental features that are not part of the standard version of JavaScript, so we need to be able to tell our linter which rules we are following in our source files.

Not only does a linter help us to make fewer errors, or at least, find those errors sooner, but it enforces some common coding style guides, which is really important, especially in big teams with many developers, each one with their favorite coding style.

It is very hard to read the code in a code base where different files, or even various functions, are written using inconsistent styles.

Installation

First of all, we have to install ESLint as follows:

```
npm install --global eslint
```

Once the executable is installed, we can run it with the following command:

```
eslint source.js
```

The output will tell us if there are errors within the file.

When we install and run it for the first time, we do not see any errors because it is completely configurable and it does not come with any default rules.

Configuration

Let's start configuring it.

ESLint can be configured using a .eslintrc file that lives in the root folder of the project.

To add some rules, we use the rules key.

For example, let's create a .eslintrc and disable the semicolon:

```
{
  "rules": {
    "semi": [2, "never"]
  }
}
```

This configuration file needs a bit of explanation: "semi" is the name of the rule and [2, "never"] is the value. It is not very intuitive the first time you see it.

ESLint rules have three levels, which determine the severity of the problem:

- **off (or 0)**: The rule is disabled
- **warn (or 1)**: The rule is a warning
- **error (or 2)**: The rule throws an error

We are using the value 2 because we want ESLint to throw an error every time our code does not follow the rule.

The second parameter tells ESLint that we want the semicolon never to be used (the opposite is *always*).

ESLint and its plugins are very well documented and for any single rule, you can find the description of the rule and some examples of when it passes and when it fails.

Now, create a file with the following content:

```
var foo = 'bar';
```

(Note that we are using `var` here because ESLint does not know yet that we want to write code in ES2015.)

If we run `eslint index.js` we get the following:

Extra semicolon (semi)

This is great; we set up the linter and it is helping us follow our first rule.

We can enable and disable every single rule manually, or we can enable the recommended configuration in one go by putting the following code into our `.eslintrc`:

```
{
  "extends": "eslint:recommended"
}
```

The `extends` key means that we are extending the recommended rules from the ESLint configuration, but we can always override single rules manually inside our `.eslintrc` using the `rules` key, as we have done before.

Once the recommended rules are enabled and we run ESLint again, we should not receive an error for the semicolon (which is not part of the recommended configuration), but we should see the linter complaining about the fact that the `foo` variable has been declared and never used.

The *no-unused-vars* rule is pretty useful for keeping our code clean.

As we have said since the beginning, we want to write ES2015 code, but changing the code to the following returns an error:

```
const foo = 'bar'
```

This is the error in question:

```
Parsing error: The keyword 'const' is reserved
```

So, to enable ES2015, we have to add a configuration option:

```
"parserOptions": {
  "ecmaVersion": 6,
}
```

Once we have done this, we will get the unused error again, which is fine.

Finally, to enable JSX, we use the following:

```
"parserOptions": {
  "ecmaVersion": 6,
  "ecmaFeatures": {
    "jsx": true
  }
},
```

At this point, if you have written any React applications before and have never used a linter, a good exercise to learn the rules and get used to it is to run ESLint against the source and fix all the issues.

There are different ways in which we make ESLint help us write better code. One is what we have done until now: run it from the command line and get the list of errors.

This works, but it is not very convenient to run it manually all the time. It would be great to add the linting process inside our editor to get immediate feedback as soon as we type. To do that, there are ESLint plugins for SublimeText, Atom, and the other most popular editors.

In the real world, running ESLint manually or getting the feedback live in the editor, even if it is very useful, is not enough, because we can miss some warnings or errors, or we can simply ignore them.

To avoid having unlinted code in our repository, what we can do is to add ESLint at one point of our process. For example, we could run the linting at test time in a such way that if the code does not pass the linting rules, the whole test step fails.

Another solution is to add the linting before opening a pull request so that we have the chance to clean up the code before our colleagues start reviewing it.

React plugin

As mentioned previously, one of the main reasons ESLint is popular is because it is extensible with plugins, the most important one for us is `eslint-plugin-react`.

ESLint can parse JSX without any plugins (just by enabling the flag), but we want to do more. For example, we may want to enforce one of the best practices we have seen in the previous section and keep our templates consistent across developers and teams.

To use the plugin, we first have to install it:

```
npm install --global eslint-plugin-react
```

Once it is installed, we instruct ESLint to use it by adding the following line to the configuration file:

```
"plugins": [
  "react"
]
```

As you can see, it is pretty straightforward, and it does not require any complex configuration or set up. Just like ESLint, without any rules it does not do anything, but we can enable the recommended configuration to activate a basic set of rules.

To do that, we update the `"extends"` key in our `.eslintrc` file as follows:

```
"extends": [
  "eslint:recommended",
  "plugin:react/recommended"
],
```

Now if we write something wrong, for example, we try to use the same prop twice in a React component, we are going to get an error:

```
<Foo bar bar />
```

The preceding code returns the following:

```
No duplicate props allowed (react/jsx-no-duplicate-props)
```

There are a lot of rules available to be used in our project. Let's go through some of them and see how they can help us to follow the best practices.

As discussed in the previous chapter, it is very helpful to indent our JSX following the tree structure of the elements, to improve the readability.

The problem comes when the indentation is not consistent through the code base and components.

So, here is an example of how ESLint can be useful to help everyone in the team follow a style guide without having to memorize it.

Notice how in this case, having the wrong indentation is not an actual error and the code works; it is just a matter of consistency.

First of all, we have to activate the rule:

```
"rules": {
  "react/jsx-indent": [2, 2]
}
```

The first 2 means that we want ESLint to raise an error in case the rule is not followed within the code, and the second 2 means that we want every JSX element to be indented with two spaces. ESLint does not make any decisions for you so it is up to you to decide which rules to enable. You can even choose to force a non-indentation using 0 as a second parameter.

Write something like the following:

```
<div>
<div />
</div>
```

ESLint complains, as follows:

```
Expected indentation of 2 space characters but found 0
(react/jsx-indent)
```

A similar rule regards the way we indent our attributes when we write them on a new line.

As we have seen in the previous section, when the attributes are too many or too long, it is a good practice to write them on a new line.

To enforce formatting where the attributes are indented by two spaces in relation to the element name, we can just enable the following rule:

```
"react/jsx-indent-props": [2, 2]
```

From now on, if we do not indent the attributes with two spaces, ESLint will fail.

The question is, when do we consider a line too long? How many attributes are too many? Every developer will have a different opinion about this. ESLint helps us to maintain consistency with the `jsx-max-props-per-line` rule so that every component is written in the same way.

The React plugin for ESLint not only gives us some rules to write better JSX, but also some rules to write better React components.

For example, we can enable a rule to enforce the sorting of the prop types into alphabetical order, a rule to give us an error when we are using a prop that has not been declared, a rule to force us to prefer stateless functional components over classes (we will see the difference in detail in `Chapter 3`, *Create Truly Reusable Components*), and so on.

Airbnb configuration

We have seen how ESLint can help us find errors using static analysis and how it can force us to follow a consistent style guide across the code base.

We have also seen how it is flexible and how we can extend it with configuration and plugins.

We know that we have recommended configurations to activate a base set of rules and avoid doing it manually, which can be a tedious task.

Let's go a step further.

The ESLint `extends` attribute is so powerful that you can use a third-party configuration as a starting point and then add your specific rules on top of it.

One of the most popular configurations used in the React world is without any doubt the Airbnb one. Developers at Airbnb created a set of rules which follows the best practice of React, and you can easily use it in your code base so that you do not have to decide manually which rules to enable.

In order to use it, you must first install some dependencies:

```
npm install --global eslint-config-airbnbeslint@^2.9.0 eslint-plugin-
jsx-a11y@^1.2.0 eslint-plugin-import@^1.7.0 eslint-plugin-react@^5.0.1
```

Then add the following configuration to your `.eslintrc`:

```
{
    "extends": "airbnb"
}
```

Try to run ESLint again against your React source files and you will see if your code follows the Airbnb rules and if you like them.

That is the easiest and most common way to get started with linting.

The basics of functional programming

Apart from following the best practices when we write JSX and use a linter to enforce consistency and find errors earlier, there is one more thing we can do to clean up our code: follow a **Functional Programming (FP)** style.

As discussed in `Chapter 1`, *Everything You Should Know About React*, React has a declarative programming approach that makes our code more readable.

Functional Programming is a declarative paradigm, where side-effects are avoided and data is considered immutable to make the code easier to maintain and to reason about.

Don't consider the following section an exhaustive guide to functional programming; it is only an introduction to get started with some concepts that are commonly used in React and of which you should be aware.

First-class objects

In JavaScript, functions are *first-class objects*, which means that they can be assigned to variables and passed as parameters to other functions.

This allows us to introduce the concept of **Higher-order Functions (HoF)**. HoFs are functions that take a function as a parameter, optionally some other parameters, and return a function. The returned function is usually enhanced with some special behaviors.

Let's look at a simple example where there is a function for adding two numbers and it gets enhanced with a function that first logs all the parameters and then executes the original one:

```
const add = (x, y) => x + y
```

```
const log = func => (...args) => {
  console.log(...args)
  return func(...args)
}

const logAdd = log(add)
```

This concept is pretty important to understand because in the React world, a common pattern is to use **Higher-order Components (HoC)**, treating our components as functions, and enhancing them with common behaviors. We will see HoCs and other patterns in Chapter 4, *Compose All the Things*.

Purity

An important aspect of FP is to write pure functions. You will encounter this concept very often in the React ecosystem, especially if you look into libraries such as Redux.

What does it mean for a function to be pure?

A function is pure when there are no sideeffects, which means that the function does not change anything that is not local to the functions itself.

For example, a function that changes the state of an application, or modifies variables defined in the upper scope, or a function that touches external entities, such as the DOM, is considered impure.

Impure functions are harder to debug and most of the time it is not possible to apply them multiple times and expect to get the same result.

For example, the following function is pure:

```
const add = (x, y) => x + y
```

It can be run multiple times, always getting the same result, because nothing is stored anywhere and nothing gets modified.

The following function is not pure:

```
let x = 0
const add = y => (x = x + y)
```

Running add(1) twice, we get two different results. The first time we get 1, but the second time we get 2, even if we call the same function with the same parameter. The reason we get that behavior is that the global state gets modified after every execution.

Immutability

We have seen how to write pure functions that don't mutate the state, but what if we need to change the value of a variable? In FP, a function, instead of changing the value of a variable, creates a new variable with a new value and returns it. This way of working with data is called **immutability**.

An immutable value is a value that cannot be changed.

Let's look at an example:

```
const add3 = arr => arr.push(3)
const myArr = [1, 2]
add3(myArr) // [1, 2, 3]
add3(myArr) // [1, 2, 3, 3]
```

The preceding function doesn't follow immutability because it changes the value of the given array. Again, if we call the same function twice, we get different results.

We can change the preceding function to make it immutable using concat, which returns a new array without modifying the given one:

```
const add3 = arr => arr.concat(3)
const myArr = [1, 2]
const result1 = add3(myArr) // [1, 2, 3]
const result2 = add3(myArr) // [1, 2, 3]
```

After we have run the function twice, myArr still has its original value.

Currying

A common technique in FP is currying. **Currying** is the process of converting a function that takes multiple arguments into a function that takes one argument at a time, returning another function. Let's look at an example to clarify the concept.

Let's start with the add function we have seen before and transform it into a curried function.

Instead of writing:

```
const add = (x, y) => x + y
```

We define the function like this:

```
const add = x => y => x + y
```

And we use it in the following way:

```
constadd1 = add(1)
add1(2) // 3
add1(3) // 4
```

This is a pretty convenient way of writing functions because since the first value is stored after the application of the first parameter, we can reuse the second function multiple times.

Composition

Finally, an important concept in FP that can be applied to React is composition. Functions (and components) can be combined to produce new functions with more advanced features and properties.

Consider the following functions:

```
const add = (x, y) => x + y
const square = x => x * x
```

These functions can be composed together to create a new function that adds two numbers and then doubles the result:

```
const addAndSquare = (x, y) => square(add(x, y))
```

Following this paradigm, we end up with small, simple, testable pure functions that can be composed together.

FP and user interfaces

The last step to take is to learn how we can use FP to build UIs, which is what we use React for.

We can think about a UI as a function to which is applied the state of the application, as follows:

```
UI = f(state)
```

We expect this function to be idempotent, so that it returns the same UI given the same state of the application.

Using React, we create our UIs using components we can consider functions, as we will see in the following chapters.

Components can be composed to form the final UI, which is a property of FP.

There are a lot of similarities in the way we build UIs with React and the principles of FP, and the more we are aware of it, the better our code will be.

Summary

In this chapter, we learned a great deal about how JSX works and how to use it in the right way in our components. We started from the basics of the syntax to create a solid knowledge base that will enable us to master JSX and its features.

In the second part, we looked at how ESLint and its plugins can help us find problems faster and enforce a consistent style guide across our code base.

Finally, we went through the basics of functional programming to understand the important concepts to use when writing a React application.

Now that our code is clean, we are ready to start digging deeper into React and learn how to write truly reusable components.

3
Create Truly Reusable Components

To create truly reusable components we have to understand the different possibilities that React gives us for defining components and when it is better to choose one or another. A new type of component has been introduced in React which lets us declare a component as a **stateless function**. It is crucial to understand this component and learn when and why it should be used.

You may have already utilized the internal state of components, but you may still be unclear about when it should be used and the problems it can give us. The best way to learn is by seeing examples, and we will do that by starting from a component which serves a single purpose and transforming it into a reusable one.

Let's first take a step back and revisit the basic concepts, so that we can move forward and create a living style guide of components by the end of this chapter.

In this chapter we will see:

- The different ways we can follow to create React components and when we should use one rather than the other
- What the stateless functional components are, and what's the difference between functional and stateful ones
- How the state works and when to avoid using it
- Why it is important to define clear prop types for each component and how to generate documentation dynamically from them with **React Docgen**
- A real example of transforming a coupled component into a reusable one
- How we can create a living style guide to document our collection of reusable components using **React Storybook**

Creating classes

We have seen in the first chapter how React uses elements to display the components on the screen.

Let's now look at the different ways in which we can define our components with React and the reasons why we should use one or other technique.

Again this book assumes that you've already played with React in a small/medium application which means that you must have created some components before.

You may have chosen one method according to the examples on the React website or by following the style of the boilerplate you used to scaffold the project.

Concepts such as props, state, and life cycle methods should be clear at this point, and we are not going to look at them in detail.

The createClass factory

Looking at the React documentation (at the time of writing), the first example we find shows us how to define components using `React.createClass`.

Let's start with a very simple snippet:

```
const Button = React.createClass({
  render() {
    return <button />
  },
})
```

With the code above we created a button, and we can reference it inside other components in our application.

We can change the snippet to use plain JavaScript as follows:

```
const Button = React.createClass({
  render() {
    return React.createElement('button')
  },
})
```

We can run the code everywhere without needing to use **Babel** for transpiling, which is a good way to start with React, avoiding the effort of learning different tools in the React ecosystem.

Extending React.Component

The second way to define a React component is by using the ES2015 classes. The `class` keyword is widely supported in modern browsers but we can safely transpile it with Babel, which supposedly, we already have in our stack if we are writing JSX.

Let's see what it means to create the same button from the example above using a class:

```
class Button extends React.Component {
  render() {
    return <button />
  }
}
```

This new way to define a component was released with React 0.13, and Facebook developers are pushing the community to use it. For example, Dan Abramov, an active member of the community and a Facebook employee recently said:

> *"ES6 classes: better the devil that's standardized" while talking about createClass vs extends Component.*

They want developers to use the latter since it's an ES2015 standard feature while `createClass` factory is not.

The main differences

Apart from the discrepancies regarding the syntax, there are some major differences that we have to keep in mind when you decide to use one or another.

Let's go through all of them in detail so you can have all the information you need to choose the best way for the needs of your team and your projects.

Props

The first difference is in how we can define the props that a component expects to receive and the default values for each one of the props.

We will see how props work in detail further in this chapter, so let's now concentrate on how we can simply define them.

With `createClass`, we declare the props inside the object that we pass as a parameter to the function, and we use the `getDefaultProps` function to return the default values:

```
const Button = React.createClass({
  propTypes: {
    text: React.PropTypes.string,
  },

  getDefaultProps() {
    return {
      text: 'Click me!',
    }
  },

  render() {
    return <button>{this.props.text}</button>
  },
})
```

As you can see, we use the `propTypes` attribute to list all the props that we can pass to the component.

We then use the `getDefaultProps` function to define the values that the props are going to have by default and which will be overwritten by the props passed from the parent, if they are present.

To achieve the same result using classes, we have to use a slightly different structure:

```
class Button extends React.Component {
  render() {
    return <button>{this.props.text}</button>
  }
}

Button.propTypes = {
  text: React.PropTypes.string,
}

Button.defaultProps = {
  text: 'Click me!',
}
```

Since **Class Properties** are still in draft (they are not part of the ECMAScript standard yet), to define the properties of the class we have to set the attributes on the class itself after it has been created.

As you can see in the example, the `propTypes` object is the same we used with `createClass`.

When it comes to setting the default props instead, we used to use a function to return the default properties object, but with classes we have to define a `defaultProps` attribute on the class and assign the default props to it.

The good thing about using classes is that we just define properties on the JavaScript object without having to use React-specific functions such as `getDefaultProps`.

State

Another big difference between the `createClass` factory and the `extends` `React.Component` method, is the way you define the initial state of the components.

Again, with `createClass` we use a function, while with the ES2015 classes we set an attribute of the instance.

Let's see an example of that:

```
const Button = React.createClass({
  getInitialState() {
    return {
      text: 'Click me!',
    }
  },

  render() {
    return <button>{this.state.text}</button>
  },
})
```

The `getInitialState` method expects an object with the default values for each one of the state properties.

However, with classes we define our initial state using the state attribute of the instance and setting it inside the constructor method of the class:

```
class Button extends React.Component {
  constructor(props) {
    super(props)

    this.state = {
      text: 'Click me!',
    }
```

```
  }
  render() {
    return <button>{this.state.text}</button>
  }
}
```

These two ways of defining the state are equivalent but, again, with classes we just define properties on the instance without using any React-specific APIs, which is good.

In ES2015, to use this in sub-classes, we first must call super. In the case of React we also pass the props to the parent.

Autobinding

createClass has a cool feature that is pretty convenient but it can also hide the way JavaScript works which is misleading, especially for beginners. This feature lets you create event handlers assuming that, when they get called, this references the component itself.

We will see how event handlers work in Chapter 6, *Write Code for the Browser*. For now, we are only interested in the way they are bound to the components we are defining.

Let's start with a simple example:

```
const Button = React.createClass({
  handleClick() {
    console.log(this)
  },

  render() {
    return <button onClick={this.handleClick} />
  },
})
```

With createClass, we can set an event handler in this way and rely on the fact that this inside the function refers to the component itself. Because of this we can, for example, call other methods of the same component instance. Calling this.setState() or any other functions would work as expected.

Let's now see how this works differently with classes, and what we can do to create the same behavior. We could define a component in the following way, extending React.Component:

```
class Button extends React.Component {
  handleClick() {
```

```
    console.log(this)
  }

  render() {
    return <button onClick={this.handleClick} />
  }
}
```

The result would be a `null` output in the console when the button is clicked. This is because our function gets passed to the event handler and we lose the reference to the component.

That does not mean that we cannot use event handlers with classes, we just have to bind our functions manually.

Let's see what solutions we can adopt and in which scenario we should prefer one or another.

As you probably know already, the new ES2015 arrow function automatically binds the current `this` to the body of the function.

So for example this snippet:

```
() => this.setState()
```

Gets transpiled into the following code with Babel:

```
var _this = this;

(function () {
  return _this.setState();
});
```

As you can imagine, one possible solution to the **autobinding** problem is using the arrow function, let's see an example:

```
class Button extends React.Component {
  handleClick() {
    console.log(this)
  }

  render() {
    return <button onClick={() => this.handleClick()} />
  }
}
```

This would work as expected without any particular problems. The only downside is that if we care about performance we have to understand what the code is doing.

Binding a function inside the render method has, in fact, an unexpected side-effect because the arrow function gets fired every time the component is rendered (which happens multiple times during the lifetime of the application).

Firing a function inside the render multiple times, even if it is not optimal, it is not a problem by itself.

The issue is that, if we are passing the function down to a child component, it receives a new prop on each update which leads to inefficient rendering, and that represents a problem, especially if the component is pure (we will talk about performance in Chapter 9, *Improve the Performance of Your Applications*).

The best way to solve it is to bind the function inside the construction in a way that it doesn't ever change even if the component renders multiple times:

```
class Button extends React.Component {
  constructor(props) {
    super(props)

    this.handleClick = this.handleClick.bind(this)
  }

  handleClick() {
    console.log(this)
  }

  render() {
    return <button onClick={this.handleClick} />
  }
}
```

That's it, problem solved!

Stateless functional components

There is one more way to define our components, and it is very different from the previous two.

This method has been introduced in **React 0.14**, and it is very powerful because it makes the code easier to maintain and reuse.

Let's see how it works and what it provides first, and then we will dig into the cases where one solution fits better than another.

The syntax is particularly terse and elegant; let's see an example:

```
() => <button />
```

The code above creates an empty button and, thanks to the concise arrow function syntax, it is straightforward and expressive. As you can see, instead of using the `createClass` factory or extending the Component, we only define a function that returns the elements to be displayed.

We can of course use the JSX syntax inside the body of the function.

Props and context

Components that are not able to receive any props from the parents are not particularly useful, and the stateless functional components can receive props as parameters:

```
props => <button>{props.text}</button>
```

Alternatively, we can use an even more concise syntax with the ES2015 destructuring:

```
({ text }) => <button>{text}</button>
```

We can define the props so that a stateless function can receive using the `propTypes` attribute in a similar way as we do when we extend components:

```
const Button = ({ text }) => <button>{text}</button>

Button.propTypes = {
  text: React.PropTypes.string,
}
```

Stateless functional components also receive a second parameter which represents the context:

```
(props, context) => (
  <button>{context.currency}{props.value}</button>
)
```

The this keyword

One thing that makes the stateless functional components different from their stateful counterparts is the fact that `this` does not represent the component during their execution.

For this reason it is not possible to use functions like `setState` or lifecycle methods that are associated with the component instance.

State

The name stateless tells us clearly that the stateless functional components do not have any internal state, and the fact that this does not exist enforces it. That makes them extremely powerful and easy to use at the same time.

The stateless functional components only receive props (and context), and they return the elements. This should remind us of the principles of *Functional Programming* that we saw in the second chapter.

Lifecycle

Stateless functional components do not provide any lifecycle hooks such as `componentDidMount`; they just implement a render-like method, and everything else has to be handled by the parent.

Refs and event handlers

Since there is no component instance, to use refs or event handlers with stateless functional components, you can define them in the following way:

```
() => {
  let input

  const onClick = () => input.focus()

  return (
    <div>
      <input ref={el => (input = el)} />
      <button onClick={onClick}>Focus</button>
    </div>
  )
}
```

No reference to component

Another difference of the stateless functional components is that, whenever we render them using the ReactTestUtils (we will cover tests extensively in Chapter 10, *About Testing and Debugging*), we do not receive back any reference to the component.

For example:

```
const Button = React.createClass({
  render() {
    return <button />
  },
})

const component = ReactTestUtils.renderIntoDocument(<Button />)
```

In this case, the component represents our Button.

```
const Button = () => <button />
const component = ReactTestUtils.renderIntoDocument(<Button />)
```

But in this case, the component is null and one solution is to wrap our component inside a <div> as follows:

```
const component = ReactTestUtils.renderIntoDocument
(<div><Button/></div>)
```

Optimization

One thing we should keep in mind when we use stateless functional components is that, even if Facebook developers say that in the future they would be able to provide performance optimizations for components without a state, at the time of writing, they perform a little bit less well.

In fact, the shouldComponentUpdate function does not exist, and there is not a way to tell React that a functional component should not be rendered if the props (or a particular prop) are not changed.

This is not a big issue, but it is something to consider.

The state

We have seen how to create a component with the factory, extending the React class or using stateless functional components.

Let's now go deeper into the topic of state and see exactly why it is important to use it and find out how it works.

We will learn when we should use stateless functions rather than stateful components and why that represents a fundamental decision in designing components.

External libraries

First of all, it is important to understand why we should consider using the state inside our components and why it can help us in different ways.

Most of the tutorials or boilerplates for React, already include external libraries to manage the state of the application, such as **Redux** or **MobX**.

This leads to a common misconception for which you cannot write a stateful application using React only, which is far from the truth.

The direct consequence is that many developers try to learn React and Redux together, so they never find out how to use the React state correctly.

This section is our opportunity to make it clear how we can use the state in the right way and understand why, in some cases, we do not need any external libraries.

How it works

Apart from the differences in declaring the initial state using the factory or extending the Component, the important concept we've learned is that each stateful React component can have an initial state.

During the lifetime of the component, the state can be modified multiple times using `setState` inside lifecycle methods or event handlers. Every time the state changes, React renders the component again with the new state, which is why documentation often says that a React component is similar to a state machine.

When the `setState` method is called with a new state (or part of it), the object gets merged into the current state. For example, if we have an initial state as the following one:

```
this.state = {
  text: 'Click me!',
}
```

And we run `setState` with a new parameter:

```
this.setState({
  cliked: true,
})
```

The resulting state is:

```
{
  cliked: true,
  text: 'Click me!',
}
```

Every time the state changes React runs the render function again, so there's no need for us to do anything other than setting the new state.

However, in some cases, we may want to perform some operations when the state is updated, and React provides a callback for that:

```
this.setState({
  clicked: true,
}, () => {
  console.log('the state is now', this.state)
})
```

If we pass any function as a second parameter of the `setState`, it gets fired when the state is updated, and the component has been rendered.

Asynchronous

The `setState` function should always be considered asynchronous, as the official documentation says:

> *There is no guarantee of synchronous operation of calls to setState [...]*

In fact, If we try to log the current value of the state into the console after we fire `setState` in an event handler, we get the old state value:

```
handleClick() {
  this.setState({
    clicked: true,
  })
  console.log('the state is now', this.state)
}

render() {
  return <button onClick={this.handleClick}>Click me!</button>
}
```

For example, the snippet above renders

the state is now null

Into the console. The reason why this happens is that React knows how to optimize the state update inside event handlers and it batches the operation for better performance.

However, if we change our code a little:

```
handleClick() {
  setTimeout(() => {
    this.setState({
      clicked: true,
    })

    console.log('the state is now', this.state)
  })
}
```

The result is going to be:

the state is now Object {clicked: true}

This is what we may have expected in the first place, and it's because React does not have any way to optimize the execution and it tries to update the state as soon as possible.

Please notice that `setTimeout` has been used in the example only to show the behavior of React but you should never write event handlers in that way.

React lumberjack

As we have said before, React works like a state machine, and it re-renders every time the state changes. Thanks to that we can go back and forth over time applying and un-applying the variations of the state, which can be very useful for debugging.

There is a library which is incredibly useful for understanding that, and it is called react-lumberjack. Its creator, Ryan Florence, is the co-creator of one of the most popular React libraries: react-router.

Using react-lumberjack is very simple, but you should remember to disable it in production. It can be installed and imported like any other npm package, or it can be utilized directly from unpkg.com in the following way:

```
<script src="https://unpkg.com/react-lumberjack@1.0.0"></script>
```

When the script is loaded, we just use our app and let the components modify their state.

If something goes wrong or we want to debug a particular state of the application we can now open the console, and write:

```
Lumberjack.back()
```

For going back in time and un-applying the state that has been changed, use the following:

```
Lumberjack.forward()
```

For going forward in time and re-applying the state.

The library is experimental and it may disappear or become part of the React Developer Tools in the near future, we mentioned it to give you a practical example of how the state works.

Using the state

Now that we know how the state works it is important to understand when it should be used and when we should avoid storing a value in the state.

If we follow the rules, we can easily figure out whenever a component should be stateless or stateful and how to deal with the state to make our component reusable across the application.

First of all, we should always keep in mind that only the minimal amount of data needed should be put into the state.

For example, if we have to change a label when a button is clicked we should not store the text of the label, but we should only save a Boolean flag that tells us if the button has been clicked or not.

In that way, we are using the state properly, and we can always recalculate different values according to it.

Secondly, we should add to the state only the values that we want to update when an event happens, and for which we want to make the component re-render.

The `isClicked` flag is an example of that, and another one could be the value of an input field before it gets submitted.

In general, we should store into the state only information needed to keep track of the current user interface state, such as the currently selected tab of a tabbed menu.

Another way to figure out whether the state is the right place to store information is to check if the data we are persisting is needed outside the component itself or by its children.

If multiple components need to keep track of the same information, we should consider using a state manager like Redux at the application level.

We will now look at the cases where we should avoid using the state if we want to follow best practice guidelines:

Derivables

Every time we can compute the final value from the props, we should not store any data into the state.

So for example, if we receive the currency and the price from the props, and we always show them together, we may think that it would be better to store it in the state and use the state value inside the render as follows:

```
class Price extends React.Component {
  constructor(props) {
    super(props)

    this.state = {
      price: `${props.currency}${props.value}`
    }
  }
}
```

```
  render() {
    return <div>{this.state.price}</div>
  }
}
```

This would work if we create it like this in the parent component:

```
<Price currency="£" value="100" />
```

The problem is that if the currency or the value change during the lifetime of the `Price` component, the state never gets recalculated (because the constructor is called once) and the application shows the wrong price.

Therefore, we should use the props to calculate a value whenever we can.

As we saw in the previous chapter, we could use a helper function directly in our render method:

```
getPrice() {
  return `${this.props.currency}${this.props.value}`
}
```

The render method

We should always keep in mind that setting the state causes the component to re-render and, for that reason, we should store into the state only values that we are using inside the render method.

For example, if we need to persist API subscriptions or timeout variables that we use inside our components but that do not affect the render in any way, we should consider keeping them in a separate module.

The following code is wrong because we are storing a value in the state to use it later but we do not access it in our render method, and we fire an unnecessary render when we set the new state:

```
componentDidMount() {
  this.setState({
    request: API.get(...)
  })
}

componentWillUnmount() {
  this.state.request.abort()
}
```

In a scenario like the previous one, it would be preferable to keep the API request stored in an external module.

Another common solution for this kind of situation is to storing the request as a private member of the component instance:

```
componentDidMount() {
    this.request = API.get(...)
}

componentWillUnmount() {
    this.request.abort()
}
```

In that way, the request is encapsulated into the component without affecting the state, so it does not trigger any additional rendering when the value changes.

The following cheat sheet from Dan Abramov will help you taking the right decision:

```
function shouldIKeepSomethingInReactState() {
    if (canICalculateItFromProps()) {
        // Don't duplicate data from props in state.
        // Calculate what you can in render() method.
        return false;
    }
    if (!amIUsingItInRenderMethod()) {
        // Don't keep something in the state
        // if you don't use it for rendering.
        // For example, API subscriptions are
        // better off as custom private fields
        // or variables in external modules.
        return false;
    }
    // You can use React state for this!
    return true;
}
```

Prop types

Our goal is to write truly reusable components and to do that we have to define their interface in the clearest possible way.

If we want our components to be reused across the application, it is crucial to make sure that our components and their parameters are well-defined and straightforward to use.

With React, there is a powerful tool that lets us express, in a very simple way, the name of the props that a component expects to receive and some validation rules for each one of them.

The rules relate to the type of the property as well as to whether the property is optional or required. There is also the option to write custom validation functions.

Let's start with a very simple example:

```
const Button = ({ text }) => <button>{text}</button>

Button.propTypes = {
  text: React.PropTypes.string,
}
```

In the snippet above, we created a stateless functional component that receives a text prop of type string.

Great, now every developer that comes across our component knows how to use it in the right way.

However, adding the property only sometimes is not enough because it does not tell us if the component works without the prop.

The button, for example, does not operate properly without text and the solution is to mark the prop as required:

```
Button.propTypes = {
  text: React.PropTypes.string.isRequired,
}
```

If a developer uses the button inside another component without setting the text property, they receive the following warning in the browser console:

```
Failed prop type: Required prop `text` was not specified
in `Button`.
```

It is important to say that the warning is emitted only in development mode. In the production version of React, the `propTypes` validation is disabled for performance reasons.

React provides ready-to-use validators for various numbers of types: from arrays to numbers, to components.

It gives us also some utilities, like **oneOf**, that accept an array of types which are valid for a particular property.

It is important to keep in mind that we should always try to pass primitive props to components because they are simpler to validate and to compare (we will see the benefits in Chapter 10, *About Testing and Debugging*).

Passing single primitive props helps us to find whether a component surface is too wide and whether it should be split into smaller surfaces.

If we realize that we are declaring too many props for a single component, and they are not related to each other, it may be better to create multiple vertical components, each one with fewer props and responsibilities.

However, in some case is unavoidable to pass objects and in those cases, we should declare our propType using shapes.

The shape function lets us declare objects with nested properties and, for each one of those, we can define their types.

For example, if we are creating a Profile component that needs a user object with a required name and an optional surname we can define it as follows:

```
const Profile = ({ user }) =>(
  <div>{user.name} {user.surname}</div>
)

Profile.propTypes = {
  user: React.PropTypes.shape({
    name: React.PropTypes.string.isRequired,
    surname: React.PropTypes.string,
  }).isRequired,
}
```

If none of the existing React propTypes satisfies our need, we can create a custom function to validate a property:

```
user: React.PropTypes.shape({
  age: (props, propName) => {
    if (!(props[propName] > 0 && props[propName] < 100)) {
      return new Error(`${propName} must be between 1 and 99`)
    }
    return null
  },
})
```

For example, in the snippet above we validate if the age field fits inside a certain range; and if it doesn't, an error is returned.

React Docgen

Now that the boundaries of our component are well-defined thanks to the prop types there is another operation that we can do to make them easy to use and share.

Of course, if our prop types have clear name and types, that should be sufficient for developers to use them, but we can do more:

We can automatically create documentation for our components starting from the definition of the prop types.

To do this there is a library called `react-docgen` that we can install with the following command:

```
npm install --global react-docgen
```

React Docgen reads the source code of our component and extracts the relevant information from the prop types and their comments.

For example, if we go back to the first button we created:

```
const Button = ({ text }) => <button>{text}</button>

Button.propTypes = {
  text: React.PropTypes.string,
}
```

And then run:

```
react-docgen button.js
```

We get the following object in return:

```
{
    "description": "",
    "methods": [],
    "props": {
        "text": {
            "type": {
                "name": "string"
            },
            "required": false,
            "description": ""
```

```
            }
        }
    }
```

Which is a JSON object that represents the interface of our components. As you can see, there is a props attribute which has our text property of type string defined inside it.

Let's see if we can do even better adding comments:

```
/**
 * A generic button with text.
 */
const Button = ({ text }) => <button>{text}</button>

Button.propTypes = {
  /**
   * The text of the button.
   */
  text: React.PropTypes.string,
}
```

If we run the command again, the result is:

```
{
    "description": "A generic button with text.",
    "methods": [],
    "props": {
        "text": {
            "type": {
                "name": "string"
            },
            "required": false,
            "description": "The text of the button."
        }
    }
}
```

We can now use the returned object to create the documentation and share it across our team or publish it on GitHub.

The fact that the output is in JSON makes the tool very flexible because it is very easy to generate web pages applying JSON objects to templates.

A real world example of components documented using docgen is the great Material UI library, where all the docs are automatically generated from the source code.

Reusable components

We have seen what are the best ways to create components and the scenarios where it makes sense to use a local state. We have also seen how we can make our components reusable defining a clear interface with prop types.

Let's now dive into a real world example and take a look at how we can transform a non-reusable component into a reusable one with a generic and cleaner interface.

Suppose we have a component that loads a collection of posts from an API endpoint, and it shows the list on the screen.

It is a simplified example, but it is useful for understanding the necessary steps we need to take to make components reusable.

The component is defined as follows:

```
class PostList extends React.Component
```

With the constructor and a life cycle method:

```
constructor(props) {
  super(props)

  this.state = {
    posts: [],
  }
}

componentDidMount() {
  Posts.fetch().then(posts => {
    this.setState({ posts })
  })
}
```

An empty array gets assigned to posts to represent the initial state.

During `componentDidMount`, the API call gets fired, and as soon as the data is available, the posts are stored in the state.

This is a very common data fetching pattern, and we will see the other possible approaches in `Chapter 5`, *Proper Data Fetching*.

Posts is a helper class that we use to communicate with the API, and it has a fetch method which returns a Promise that gets resolved with a list of posts.

We can now move into the part where the posts are displayed:

```
render() {
  return (
    <ul>
      {this.state.posts.map(post => (
        <li key={post.id}>
          <h1>{post.title}</h1>
          {post.excerpt && <p>{post.excerpt}</p>}
        </li>
      ))}
    </ul>
  )
}
```

Inside the `render` method, we loop through the posts, and we map each one of them into a `<li>` element.

We assume that the title field is always present, and we show it inside an `<h1>` while the excerpt is optional, and we show it inside a paragraph only if it exists.

The above component works fine, and it has no problems.

Now, suppose that we need to render a similar list but this time, we want to display a list of users received from the props rather than the state (to make clear that we can serve different scenarios):

```
const UserList = ({ users }) => (
  <ul>
    {users.map(user => (
      <li key={user.id}>
        <h1>{user.username}</h1>
        {user.bio && <p>{user.bio}</p>}
      </li>
    ))}
  </ul>
)
```

Given a collection of users, the code above renders an unordered list very similar to the posts one.

The differences are that the heading, in this case, is the username rather than title and the optional field, that has to be shown only if present, is the bio of the user.

Duplicating the code is usually not the best solution so let's see how React can help us to keep our code **Don't Repeat Yourself** (**DRY**). The first step to creating a reusable List component is to abstract it a little and decouple it from the data it has to display and we do that by defining a generic collection property. The main requirement is that, for the posts, we want to display the title and the excerpt; while, for the users, we have to show the username and the bio.

For doing that, we create two props: one called `titleKey` where we specify the name of the attribute to be displayed and one called `textKey` that we use to specify the optional field.

The props of the new reusable `List` are the following:

```
List.propTypes = {
  collection: React.PropTypes.array,
  textKey: React.PropTypes.string,
  titleKey: React.PropTypes.string,
}
```

Since the `List` is not going to have any state or function, we can write it as a stateless functional component:

```
const List = ({ collection, textKey, titleKey }) => (
  <ul>
    {collection.map(item =>
      <Item
        key={item.id}
        text={item[textKey]}
        title={item[titleKey]}
      />
    )}
  </ul>
)
```

The `List` receives the props, and iterates over the collection, mapping all the items into another component (that we are going to create next). As you can see, we are passing to the children titles and text props which represent the values of the main attribute and the optional one, respectively.

The `Item` component is very simple and clean:

```
const Item = ({ text, title }) => (
  <li>
    <h1>{title}</h1>
    {text && <p>{text}</p>}
  </li>
)
```

```
Item.propTypes = {
  text: React.PropTypes.string,
  title: React.PropTypes.string,
}
```

So we've created two components with a well-defined surface area which can we use together to display posts, users or any other kinds of lists. Smaller components are better for several reasons: for example, they are more maintainable and testable which make it easier to find and fix bugs.

Great, we can now rewrite our two components, `PostsList` and `UsersList`, to make them use the generic reusable list and avoid duplicating code.

Let's modify the render method of `PostsLists` as follows:

```
render() {
  return (
    <List
      collection={this.state.posts}
      textKey="excerpt"
      titleKey="title"
    />
  )
}
```

And the `UserList` function as follows:

```
const UserList = ({ users }) => (
  <List
    collection={users}
    textKey="bio"
    titleKey="username"
  />
)
```

We went from a single-purpose component to a reusable one using the props to create a generic and well-defined interface.

It is now possible to reuse this component as many times as we need in our application and every developer can easily understand how to implement it thanks to the prop types.

We could also go a step further using `react-docgen` to document our reusable list, as we have seen in the previous section.

The benefits of using a reusable component over a component which is coupled with the data it handles are many.

Suppose, for example, that we want to add logic to hide and show the optional field only when a button is clicked.

Alternatively, perhaps there is a new requirement to add a check and, if the title attribute is longer than twenty five characters, it gets cut and hyphenate.

We can now make the change at one single point, and all the components that are using it will benefit from the modification.

Living style guides

Creating reusable components with a clear API is great to avoid duplicating code across the application, but that is not the only reason why you should focus on reusability.

In fact, creating simple and clean components that accept clear props and that are decoupled from the data is the best way to share a library of base components with the rest of the team. Your base generic and reusable components represent your palette of ready-to-use components that you can share with other developers and designers on your team.

For example, in the previous section we created a generic list with title and text, and since it is decoupled from the data it shows, we can use it many times within the app just by passing the right props. If a new list of categories has to be implemented, we just pass a collection of categories to the list component, and it's done.

The problem is that sometimes is not easy for new developers to find out if components already exist or if new ones are needed. The solution is usually to create a style guide; this is a very powerful and effective tool that allows you to share a set of elements within the team.

A style guide is a visual collection of every single component of the app that can be used across different pages. It is a really useful way to exchange information with members of the team who have different skills, keeping the style consistent as time passes and as the number of components increases.

Unfortunately, creating a style guide is not always easy in web applications because often the concerns are not well defined, and some elements get duplicated to achieve small variations in requirements. React helps us by creating well-defined components and building a style guide, so it does not require too much effort.

Not only React makes it simpler to create reusable components, but there are also tools that can help us building a visual library starting from the code of the components themselves. One of those tools is called `react-storybook`.

React Storybook isolates a component so that you can render single components without running the entire app, which is perfect for both development and testing.

As the name suggests, React Storybook lets you write stories which represent the possible states of the components. For example, if you are creating a TO-DO list, you could have a story to represent a checked item and another story to describe an unchecked one.

That is a great tool for sharing components across the team and with other developers to improve collaboration. A new developer joining the company can just look at the existing stories to figure out if there is any need to create a new component or if an existing one already provides a solution to a particular problem.

Let's apply storybook to the List example that we created in the previous chapter. First of all, we have to install the library:

```
npm install --save @kadira/react-storybook-addon
```

Once the package is installed, we can start creating a story.

Our list item has a required title attribute and an optional text, so we can create at least two stories to represent those states.

Stories usually go into a folder called `stories` that you can create inside your components folder or wherever it fits better in your folder structure.

Inside the stories folder you can create one file per component.

In this case, we'll define our stories in `list.js`.

We first import the main function from the library:

```
import { storiesOf } from '@kadira/storybook'
```

Then we use it to define our stories, as follows:

```
storiesOf('List', module)
  .add('without text field', () => (
    <List collection={posts} titleKey="title" />
  ))
```

Using `storiesOf`, we can define the name of the component and add the stories, and each one includes a description and a function that must return the component to be rendered.

Suppose that `posts` is the following collection of blog posts about React:

```
const posts = [
  {
    id: 1,
    title: 'Create Apps with No Configuration',
  },
  {
    id: 2,
    title: 'Mixins Considered Harmful',
  },
]
```

Before running storybook and navigating to our visual collection of components and stories we have to configure it.

To do that we create a folder called `.storybook` in the root folder of our application.

Inside the `.storybook` folder we create a `config.js` file to load our stories:

```
import { configure } from '@kadira/storybook'

function loadStories() {
  require('../src/stories/list')
}

configure(loadStories, module)
```

We first load the configure function from the library and then we define a function to load each single story using their paths.

Then, we pass the function to the configuration method, and we are ready to go.

The last things we have to do are to make storybook start and to access our style guide in the browser by creating an npm task that fires the storybook executable.

To do that, we just have to add this:

```
"storybook": "start-storybook -p 9001"
```

To the script section of our `package.json`.

We can now run:

```
npm run storybook
```

And point the browser to `http://localhost:9001`

We can access the Storybook interface where we can see the list of stories on the left.

When we click on one of those stories, we can see the components being rendered in the right area.

Great, we now have a living style guide to document all the states of our components that can be used to share information with designer and product managers.

As a final task, we can create a second story.

Our list can show items with title and text, so we add the second attribute to our posts collection:

```
const posts = [
  {
    id: 1,
    title: 'Create Apps with No Configuration',
    excerpt: 'Create React App is a new officially supported...',
  },
  {
    id: 2,
    title: 'Mixins Considered Harmful',
    excerpt: '"How do I share the code between several...',
  },
]
```

We can now add the story appending the following snippet right after the one we previously created:

```
.add('with text field', () => (
  <List collection={posts} titleKey="title" textKey="excerpt" />
))
```

If we now go back to the browser, the page is automatically refreshed, and we see two stories in the left sidebar.

By clicking on each one of them we can see the component updating on the right.

If we select the first one, we see the list of titles only, while if we selected the second one, we see the list of titles and excerpts.

For more complex components, you can add multiple stories and show all the possible states and variations that each component can assume.

Summary

The journey to learn how to make reusable components has come to the end.

We started from a deep study of the basics and seeing the differences between stateful and stateless components, and we saw an example of how to make a tightly coupled component reusable. We've looked at the internal state of a component and at when it is better to avoid using it. We learned the basics of prop types and applied those concepts to the reusable components we created.

Finally, we looked at how living style guides can help us to communicate better with other members of our team, to avoid creating duplicated components and to enforce consistency within the application.

We are now ready to learn the various techniques we can put in place to compose our components.

4
Compose All the Things

In the previous chapter, we saw how to create reusable components with a clean interface. Now, it is time to learn how to make those components communicate with each other effectively.

React is so powerful because it lets you build complex applications composing small, testable, and maintainable components. Applying this paradigm, you can take control of every single part of the application.

In this chapter, we will go through some of the most popular composition patterns and tools.

We will see the following:

- How components communicate with each other using props and children
- The Container and Presentational pattern and how it can make our code more maintainable
- The problem mixins tried to solve and why they failed
- What HoCs are and how we can structure our applications in a better way, thanks to them
- The recompose library with its ready-made functions
- How we can interact with the context and avoid coupling our components to it
- What is the Function as Child component pattern and what are its benefits?

Communication between components

Reusing functions is one of our goals as developers, and we have seen how React makes it easy to create reusable components.

Reusable components can be shared across multiple domains of your application to avoid duplication.

Small components with a clean interface can be composed together to create complex applications that are powerful and maintainable at the same time.

Composing React components is pretty straightforward; you just have to include them in the `render` method:

```
const Profile = ({ user }) => (
  <div>
    <Picture profileImageUrl={user.profileImageUrl} />
    <UserName name={user.name} screenName={user.screenName} />
  </div>
)

Profile.propTypes = {
  user: React.PropTypes.object,
}
```

For example, you can create a `Profile` component by simply composing a `Picture` component to display the profile image and a `UserName` component to display the name and the screen name of the user.

In this way, you can produce new parts of the user interface very quickly, writing only a few lines of code.

Whenever you compose components, as in the preceding example, you share data between them using **props**.

Props are the way a parent component can pass its data down the tree to every component that needs it (or part of it).

When a component passes some props to another component, it is called the **Owner**, irrespective of the parent-child relation between them.

For example, in the preceding snippet, `Profile` is not the direct parent of `Picture` (the `div` tag is) but `Profile` owns `Picture` because it passes down the props to it.

Children

There is a special prop that can be passed from the owners to the components defined inside their render method; it is called **children.**

In the React documentation, it is described as *opaque* because it is a property that does not tell anything about the value it contains.

Subcomponents defined inside the render method of a parent component usually receive props passed as attributes of the component itself in JSX, or as a second parameter of the `createElement` function.

Components can also be defined with nested components inside them, and they can access those children using the children prop.

Consider that we have a `Button` component that has a text property representing the text of the button:

```
const Button = ({ text }) => (
  <button className="btn">{text}</button>
)

Button.propTypes = {
  text: React.PropTypes.string,
}
```

It can be used in the following way:

```
<Button text="Click me!" />
```

And it renders the following code:

```
<button class="btn">Click me!</button>
```

Now, suppose we want to use the same button with the same class name in multiple parts of our application, and we also want to be able to display more than a simple string.

In fact, our UI consists of buttons with text, buttons with text and icons, and buttons with text and labels.

In most cases, a good solution would be to add multiple parameters to the `Button` or to create different versions of the `Button`, each one with its single specialization, for example, `IconButton`.

However, if we realize that our `Button` could be just a wrapper, and we want to be able to render any element inside it, we can use the `children` property.

We can easily do that by changing the `Button` component from the preceding example to be similar to the following snippet:

```
const Button = ({ children }) => (
  <button className="btn">{children}</button>
)

Button.propTypes = {
  children: React.PropTypes.array,
}
```

Applying this change, we are not limited to a simple single text property but we can pass any element to `Button`, and it is rendered in place of the `children` property.

In this case, any element that we wrap inside the `Button` component will be rendered as a child of the button element with the `btn` class name.

For example, if we want to render an image inside the button and a text wrapped into a span, we can do this:

```
<Button>
  <img src="..." alt="..." />
  <span>Click me!</span>
</Button>
```

The preceding snippet gets rendered in the browser as follows:

```
<button className="btn">
  <img src="..." alt="..." />
  <span>Click me!</span>
</button>
```

This is a pretty convenient way to allow components to accept any `children` elements and wrap those elements inside a predefined parent.

Now we can pass images, labels, and even other React components inside the `Button` and they will be rendered as its children.

As you can see in the preceding example, we defined the children property as an array, which means that we can pass any number or elements as the component's children.

We can pass a single child, as shown in the following code:

```
<Button>
  <span>Click me!</span>
</Button>
```

If we pass a single child, we get this:

Failed prop type: Invalid prop `children` of type `object` supplied to `Button`, expected `array`.

This is because, when a component has a single child, React optimizes the creation of the elements and avoids allocating an array for performance reasons.

We can easily fix this warning by setting the children prop to accept the following prop types:

```
Button.propTypes = {
  children: React.PropTypes.oneOfType([
    React.PropTypes.array,
    React.PropTypes.element,
  ]),
}
```

Container and Presentational pattern

In the last chapter, we saw how to take a coupled component and make it reusable step by step.

In this section, we will see how to apply a similar pattern to our components to make them more clean and maintainable.

React components typically contain a mix of **logic** and **presentation**.

By logic, we refer to anything that is unrelated to the UI, such as API calls, data manipulation, and event handlers.

The presentation is, instead, the part inside the render method where we create the elements to be displayed on the UI.

In React, there is a simple and powerful pattern, known as **Container** and **Presentational**, which we can apply when creating components that help us to separate those two concerns.

Creating well-defined boundaries between logic and presentation not only makes components more reusable, but it provides many other benefits, which you will learn about in this section.

Again, one of the best ways to learn new concepts is by seeing practical examples, so let's delve into some code.

Suppose we have a component that uses geolocation APIs to get the position of the user and displays the latitude and longitude on the page in the browser.

We first create a `geolocation.js` file in our components folder and define the `Geolocation` component using a `class`:

```
class Geolocation extends React.Component
```

We then define a `constructor`, where we initialize the internal state and bind the event handlers:

```
constructor(props) {
  super(props)

  this.state = {
    latitude: null,
    longitude: null,
  }

  this.handleSuccess = this.handleSuccess.bind(this)
}
```

Now, we can use the `componentDidMount` callback to fire the request to the APIs:

```
componentDidMount() {
  if (navigator.geolocation) {
    navigator.geolocation.getCurrentPosition(this.handleSuccess)
  }
}
```

When the browser returns the data, we store the result into the state using the following function:

```
handleSuccess({ coords }) {
  this.setState({
    latitude: coords.latitude,
    longitude: coords.longitude,
  })
}
```

Finally, we show the latitude and longitude using the `render` method:

```
render() {
  return (
    <div>
      <div>Latitude: {this.state.latitude}</div>
      <div>Longitude: {this.state.longitude}</div>
    </div>
  )
}
```

It is important to note that, during the first render, latitude and longitude are `null` because we ask the browser for the coordinates when the component is mounted. In a real-world component, you might want to display a spinner until the data gets returned; to do that, you can use one of the conditional techniques we saw in `Chapter 2`, *Clean Up Your Code*.

Now this component does not have any problems, and it works as expected.

Suppose you are working along with the designer on the UI side of the component, where latitude and longitude are displayed to the user.

Wouldn't it be nice to separate it from the part where the position gets requested and loaded in order to iterate faster on it?

Isolating the presentational part of the main component, we could render the component with fake data in a **Style Guide** using **Storybook**, as we saw in the last chapter, with all the benefits of creating reusable components.

So, let's look at how we can do it, by following the Container and Presentational pattern.

In this pattern, every component is split into two smaller ones, each one with its clear responsibilities.

The Container knows everything about the logic of the component and it's where the APIs are called. It also deals with data manipulation, and event handling.

The Presentational component is where the UI is defined, and it receives data in the form of props from the container.

Since the Presentational component is usually logic-less, we can create it as a functional stateless component.

There are no rules that say that the Presentational component must not have a state. For example, it could keep a UI state inside it.

In this case, we just need a component to display the latitude and longitude, so we are going to use a simple function.

First of all, we should rename our `Geolocation` component to `GeolocationContainer`:

```
class GeolocationContainer extends React.Component
```

We will also change the filename from `geolocation.js` to `geolocation-container.js`.

This rule is not strict, but it is best practice widely used in the React community to append Container to the end of the Container component name and give the original name to the Presentational one.

We also have to change the implementation of the render method and remove all the UI part of it, as follows:

```
render() {
  return (
    <Geolocation {...this.state} />
  )
}
```

As you can see in the snippet, instead of creating the HTML elements inside the render method of the container, we just use the Presentational one (which we will create next), and we pass the state to it.

The **state** has the latitude and longitude properties, which are `null` by default, and they contain the real position of the user when the browser has fired the **callback**.

We are using the spread attribute operator, which we saw in Chapter 2, *Clean Up Your Code*; it is a convenient way to pass the attributes of the state, avoiding writing prop by prop manually.

Let's now create a new file, called `geolocation.js`, where we define the stateless functional component as follows:

```
const Geolocation = ({ latitude, longitude }) => (
  <div>
    <div>Latitude: {latitude}</div>
    <div>Longitude: {longitude}</div>
  </div>
)
```

Stateless functional components are an incredibly elegant way to define UIs. They are pure functions that, given a state, return the elements.

In this case, our function receives the latitude and longitude from the owner, and it returns the markup structure to display it.

We surely want to follow the best practices and define a clear interface for our component, so we use `propTypes` to declare the properties that the component needs:

```
Geolocation.propTypes = {
  latitude: React.PropTypes.number,
  longitude: React.PropTypes.number,
}
```

If you run the components in the browser, you can see something like this:

Following the Container and Presentational pattern, we created a dumb reusable component that we can put in our Style Guide, passing fake coordinates to it.

If, in some other parts of the application, we need to display the same data structure, we do not have to create a new component; we just wrap this one into a new container that, for example, could load the latitude and longitude from a different endpoint.

At the same time, other developers in our team can improve the container that uses the geolocation by adding some error handling logic, without affecting the presentation.

They can even build a temporary presentational component just to display and debug data and then replace it with the real presentational component when it is ready.

Being able to work in parallel on the same component is a big win for teams, especially for those companies where building interfaces is an iterative process.

This pattern is simple but very powerful, and when applied to big applications it can make the difference when it comes to the speed of development and maintainability of the project.

On the other hand, applying this pattern without a real reason can give us the opposite problem and make the **codebase** less useful as it involves the creation of more files and components.

So, we should think carefully when we decide that a component has to be refactored following the Container and Presentational pattern.

In general, the right path to follow is starting with a single component and splitting it only when the logic and the presentation become too coupled where they shouldn't.

In our example, we began from a single component, and we realized that we could separate the API call from the markup.

Deciding what to put in the container and what goes in the presentational is not always straightforward; the following points should help you make that decision.

Container components:

- They are more concerned about the behavior
- They render their presentational components
- They make API calls and manipulate data
- They define event handlers
- They are written as classes

Presentational components:

- They are more concerned with the visual representation
- They render the HTML markup (or other components)
- They receive data from the parents in the form of props
- They are often written as stateless functional components

Mixins

Components are great to achieve reusability, but what if different components in different domains share the same behavior?

We do not want duplicated code in our applications, and React gives us a tool that we can use when we want to share functionalities across various components: **mixins**.

Using mixins is no longer recommended, but it is worth understanding the problems they tried to solve and see what the possible alternative solutions are.

Also, it could happen that you might have to work on a legacy project that uses an older version of React, and it makes sense to know what mixins are and how to deal with them.

First of all, mixins work only with the `createClass` factory, so if you are using classes, you cannot use mixins, and that is one of the reasons why their usage is discouraged.

Suppose you are using `createClass` in your application and you find yourself needing to write the same code into different components.

For example, you need to listen to the window resize event to get the size of the window and do some operations accordingly.

One way of using a mixin is to write it once and share it across the different components. Let's delve into the code.

A mixin can be defined as an object literal that has the same functions and attributes of a component:

```
const WindowResize = {...}
```

To communicate with the component, mixins usually use the state. With `getInitialState`, the state gets initialized with the initial `innerWidth` of window:

```
getInitialState() {
  return {
    innerWidth: window.innerWidth,
  }
},
```

Now we want to keep track of the changes, so when the component mounts, we start listening to the window resize event:

```
componentDidMount() {
  window.addEventListener('resize', this.handleResize)
},
```

We also want to remove the event listener as soon as the component unmounts, which is critical freeing the memory and not leaving unused listeners attached to the window:

```
componentWillUnmount() {
  window.removeEventListener('resize', this.handleResize)
},
```

Finally, we define the callback to be called every time the window resize event is fired.

The callback function is implemented to update the state with the new innerWidth component so that the component that is using the mixin re-renders itself with the fresh value available:

```
handleResize() {
  this.setState({
    innerWidth: window.innerWidth,
  })
},
```

As you can see from the preceding snippet, creating a mixin is very similar to creating a component.

Now, if we want to use the mixin in our component, we just have to assign it to the array of mixins, which is a property of the object:

```
const MyComponent = React.createClass({

  mixins: [WindowResize],

  render() {
    console.log('window.innerWidth', this.state.innerWidth)
    ...
  },

})
```

From this point on, the value of innerWidth of the window will be available in the state of our component and the component will re-render with the updated value anytime innerWidth changes.

We can use the mixin in many components at a time and also use multiple mixins for each component.

A nice feature of mixins is that they can merge lifecycle methods and the initial state.

For example, if we use our `WindowResize` mixin in a component where we also define a `componentDidMount` hook, both will be executed in order.

The same happens in the case of multiple mixins that use the same lifecycle hooks.

Let's now go through the problems of mixins and, in the next section, we will see which is the best technique to achieve the same result without all the issues.

First of all, mixins sometimes use internal functions to communicate with the component.

For example, our `WindowResize` mixin could expect the component to implement a `handleResize` function and give developers the freedom of doing some operations when the size changes instead of using the state to trigger the update.

Alternatively, instead of setting the new value into the state, the mixin could require the component to call a function, something like `getInnerWidth` in our example, to get the actual value.

Unfortunately, there is no way for us to know the list of methods that has to be implemented.

This is particularly bad for maintainability because, if a component uses multiple mixins, it ends up implementing different methods, which makes it difficult to eliminate the code when some mixins are removed, or they change their behavior.

A very common problem with mixins is clashing. In fact, though it is true that React is smart enough to merge lifecycle callbacks, it cannot do anything if two mixins define or require the same function name or use the same attribute in the state.

This is pretty bad in big codebases because it can give us unexpected behaviors and it makes it very hard to debug issues.

As we have seen in the `WindowResize` example, mixins tend to communicate with the component using the state. So, for example, a mixin can update a special attribute in the state of a component, then the component re-renders, taking into account the new attribute.

This makes components use the state even if is not needed, which is bad because we have seen that we should avoid using it as much as we can to improve reusability and maintainability.

Last but not least, sometimes it can happen that some mixins depend on other mixins. For example, we could create **ResponsiveMixin**, which changes the visibility of some components according to the size of the window, which is provided in the `WindowResize` mixin.

This coupling between mixins makes it very hard to refactor the components and scale the application.

Higher-order Components

In the previous section, we saw how mixins are useful for sharing functionalities between components and the problems that they bring to our applications.

In the Functional Programming section of `Chapter 2`, *Clean Up Your Code*, we mentioned the concept of **Higher-order Functions (HoFs)**, which are functions that, given a function, enhance it with some extra behaviors, returning a new one.

Let's see if we can apply the same concept to React components and achieve our goal to sharing functionalities between components while avoiding the downsides of mixins.

When we apply the idea of HoFs to components, we call it **Higher-order Components (HoCs)** for brevity.

First of all, let's see what a HoC looks like:

```
const HoC = Component => EnhancedComponent
```

HoCs are functions that take a component as input and return an enhanced one as the output.

Let's start with a very simple example to understand what an enhanced component looks like.

Suppose you need to attach to every component the same `className` property for some reason. You could go and change all the render methods adding the `className` prop to each of them, or you could write a HoC such as the following one:

```
const withClassName = Component => props => (
  <Component {...props} className="my-class" />
)
```

The preceding code can be a little difficult to understand initially; let's try to understand it.

We declare a `withClassName` function that takes a `Component` and returns another function.

The returned function is a stateless functional component that receives some props and renders the original component. The collected props are spread and a `className` property with the "`my-class`" value is passed to it.

The reason why HoCs usually spread the props they receive on the component is because they tend to be transparent and only add the new behavior.

This is pretty simple and not very useful, but it should give you a better understanding of what HoCs are and what they look like.

Let's now see how to use the `withClassName` HoC in our components.

First of all, we create a stateless functional component that receives the class name and applies it to a `div` tag:

```
const MyComponent = ({ className }) => (
  <div className={className} />
)

MyComponent.propTypes = {
  className: React.PropTypes.string,
}
```

Instead of using it directly, we pass it to a HoC, as follows:

```
const MyComponentWithClassName = withClassName(MyComponent)
```

Wrapping our components into the `withClassName` function, we ensure that it receives the `className` property.

Let's now move on to something more exciting and let's try to transform the `WindowResize` mixin we saw in the previous section into a HoC function that we can reuse across our application.

The mixin was simply listening to the window resize event and making the updated `innerWidth` property of the window available into the state.

One of the biggest problems with that mixin was in fact that it was using the state of the component to provide the `innerWidth` value.

Doing that is bad because it pollutes the state with additional attributes and those attributes may also clash with the attributes used in the components itself.

First of all, we have to create a function that receives a component:

```
const withInnerWidth = Component => (
  class extends React.Component { ... }
)
```

You may have spotted a pattern in the way HoCs are named. It is a common practice to prefix HoCs that provide some information to the components they enhance using the *with* pattern.

Our `withInnerWidth` function will return a class component instead of a functional stateless component because, as we saw in the previous example, we need additional functions and state.

Let's see what the returned class looks like.

In the constructor, the initial state gets defined, and the `handleResize` callback is bound to the current class:

```
constructor(props) {
  super(props)

  this.state = {
    innerWidth: window.innerWidth,
  }

  this.handleResize = this.handleResize.bind(this)
}
```

The lifecycle hooks and the event handler are identical to the mixin's:

```
componentDidMount() {
  window.addEventListener('resize', this.handleResize)
}

componentWillUnmount() {
  window.removeEventListener('resize', this.handleResize)
}

handleResize() {
  this.setState({
    innerWidth: window.innerWidth,
  })
}
```

Finally, the original component gets rendered in this way:

```
render() {
    return <Component {...this.props} {...this.state} />
}
```

As you may note here, we are spreading the props as we saw before, but we are also spreading the state.

In fact, we are storing the `innerWidth` value inside the state to achieve the original behavior, but we do not pollute the state of the component; we use props instead.

As you learned in `Chapter 3`, *Create Truly Reusable Components*, using props is always a good solution to enforce reusability.

Now, using a HoC and getting the `innerWidth` value is pretty straightforward.

We create a stateless functional component that expects `innerWidth` as property:

```
const MyComponent = ({ innerWidth }) => {
    console.log('window.innerWidth', innerWidth)
    ...
}

MyComponent.propTypes = {
    innerWidth: React.PropTypes.number,
}
```

We enhance it as follows:

```
const MyComponentWithInnerWidth = withInnerWidth(MyComponent)
```

The advantages of doing this rather than using a mixin are multiple: first of all, we do not pollute any state, and we do not require the component to implement any function.

This means that the component and the HoC are not coupled, and they can both be reused across the application.

Again, using props instead of state lets us make our component dumb so that we can use it in our Style Guide, ignoring any complex logic and just passing down the props.

In this particular case, we could create a component for each of the different `innerWidth` sizes we support.

Consider the following example:

```
<MyComponent innerWidth={320} />
```

Or:

```
<MyComponent innerWidth={960} />
```

Recompose

As soon as we become familiar with HoCs, we realize how powerful they are and how we can get the most out of them.

There is a popular library called recompose which provides many useful HoCs and also a way to compose them nicely.

The HoCs that the library offers are small utilities that we can use to wrap our components, moving away some logic from them and making them more dumb and reusable.

Consider that your component is receiving a user object from an API, and this user object has many attributes.

Letting components receive arbitrary objects is not a good practice because it relies on the fact that the component knows the shape of the object and, most importantly, if the object changes, the component breaks.

A better way for a component to receive props from the parent is to define each single property using primitives.

So, we have a `Profile` component to display `username` and `age`; it looks like this:

```
const Profile = ({ user }) => (
  <div>
    <div>Username: {user.username}</div>
    <div>Age: {user.age}</div>
  </div>
)

Profile.propTypes = {
  user: React.PropTypes.object,
}
```

If you want to change its interface to receive single props instead of the full user object, we can do it with the `flattenProp` HoC provided by recompose.

Let's see how it works.

We first change the component to declare single properties, as follows:

```
const Profile = ({ username, age }) => (
  <div>
    <div>Username: {username}</div>
    <div>Age: {age}</div>
  </div>
)

Profile.propTypes = {
  username: React.PropTypes.string,
  age: React.PropTypes.number,
}
```

Then, we enhance it with the HoC:

```
const ProfileWithFlattenUser = flattenProp('user')(Profile)
```

You may have noted here that we are using the HoC in a slightly different way. Some of them, in fact, use the partial application to receive the parameters first, which is a functional approach.

Their signature is something similar to the following:

```
const HoC = args => Component => EnhancedComponent
```

What we can do is create a function using the first call and wrap our component into it:

```
const withFlattenUser = flattenProp('user')
const ProfileWithFlattenUser = withFlattenUser(Profile)
```

Great! Now suppose for some reason we want to change the attribute username to make this component more generic and reusable.

We can use `renameProp`, which the recompose library gives us, and update our component like this:

```
const Profile = ({ name, age }) => (
  <div>
    <div>Name: {name}</div>
    <div>Age: {age}</div>
  </div>
)
```

```
Profile.propTypes = {
  name: React.PropTypes.string,
  age: React.PropTypes.number,
}
```

Now we want to apply multiple HoC components: one for flattening the user prop and one to rename a single prop from the user object, but concatenating functions does not seem a good idea.

Here is where the `compose` function of recompose comes handy.

We can, in fact, pass multiple HoCs to it and get a single enhanced HoC:

```
const enhance = compose(
  flattenProp('user'),
  renameProp('username', 'name')
)
```

Then, we can apply it to our component in the following way:

```
const EnhancedProfile = enhance(Profile)
```

This is a more convenient and elegant way.

With recompose, we are not limited to using only the HoCs provided by the library, we can use compose our HoC in the same way or even use them all together:

```
const enhance = compose(
  flattenProp('user'),
  renameProp('username', 'name'),
  withInnerWidth
)
```

As you can see here, the compose function is very powerful, and it makes the code more readable.

We can concatenate multiple HoCs to keep our components as simple as possible.

It is important not to abuse HoCs because with every abstraction come some problems; in this case, the trade-off is related to performance.

You have to think that, every time you wrap a component into a higher-order one, you are adding a new render function, a new lifecycle method call, and memory allocation.

For that reason, it is important to think carefully about when it makes sense to use HoC and when it is better to rethink your structure.

Context

HoCs come in very handy when we have to deal with context.

Context is a feature that has always been present in React, and it is used in many libraries, even if it has been documented after a little while.

The documentation still advises to use it very sparingly because it is experimental and likely to change in the future.

However, in some scenarios, it is a very powerful tool that can help us pass information down to the tree without using props at every level.

What we can do, to get the benefits of context without coupling our components to its APIs, is use a HoC.

A HoC can get the data from the context, transform it to props, and pass the props down to the component.

In this way, the component is unaware of the context, and it can be easily reused in different parts of the application.

Also, if the APIs of the context change in the future, the only part of the application that has to be changed is the HoC because the components are decoupled from it, which is a big win.

There is a function provided by recompose, which makes using context in a transparent way and receiving props very easy and straightforward; let's see how it works.

Suppose you have a `Price` component that you use to display the currency and the value.

The context is widely used to pass down common configuration from the root to the leaves and currency is one of those values.

Let's start with a context-aware component and let's transform it step by step into a reusable one, thanks to HoCs:

```
const Price = ({ value }, { currency }) => (
  <div>{currency}{value}</div>
)

Price.propTypes = {
  value: React.PropTypes.number,
}

Price.contextTypes = {
  currency: React.PropTypes.string,
```

```
  }
```

We have a stateless functional component that receives the value as a property and the currency as the second parameter from the context.

We also define the prop types and the context types for both values.

As you can see, this component is not truly reusable because it needs a parent with the currency as child context types to work.

For example, we cannot use it easily in our Style Guide, passing a fake currency as a prop.

First of all, let's change the component to get both values from the props:

```
const Price = ({ currency, value }) => (
  <div>{currency}{value}</div>
)

Price.propTypes = {
  currency: React.PropTypes.string,
  value: React.PropTypes.number,
}
```

Of course, we cannot substitute it with the previous one straightaway because no parents are setting its currency prop.

What we can do is wrap it into a HoC that can transform the values received from the context into props.

We use the `getContext` function from recompose but you can easily write a custom wrapper from scratch.

Again, we use the partial application to specialize the HoC and reuse it multiple times:

```
const withCurrency = getContext({
  currency: React.PropTypes.string
})
```

And then we apply it to the component:

```
const PriceWithCurrency = withCurrency(Price)
```

Now, we can replace the old `Price` component with the resulting one, and it will still work without being coupled with the context.

That is a big win because we did not have to change the parent, we can use the context without worrying about future API changes, and the `Price` component is now reusable.

In fact, we can pass arbitrary currencies and values to the component without needing a custom parent to provide the values.

Function as Child

There is a pattern that is gaining consensus within the React community, called **Function as Child**.

It is widely used in the popular library react-motion, which we will see in `Chapter 6`, *Write Code for the Browser*.

The main concept is that, instead of passing a child in the form of a component, we define a function that can receive parameters from the parent.

Let's see what it looks like:

```
const FunctionAsChild = ({ children }) => children()

FunctionAsChild.propTypes = {
  children: React.PropTypes.func.isRequired,
}
```

As you can see, `FunctionAsChild` is a component that has a children property defined as a function and, instead of being used as a JSX expression, it gets called.

The preceding component can be used in the following way:

```
<FunctionAsChild>
  {() => <div>Hello, World!</div>}
</FunctionAsChild>
```

It is as simple as it looks: the children function is fired in the render method of the parent and it returns the `Hello, World!` text wrapped in a `div`, which is displayed on the screen.

Let's delve into a more meaningful example where the parent component passes some parameters to the children function.

Create a `Name` component that expects a function as children and passes it the string `World`:

```
const Name = ({ children }) => children('World')

Name.propTypes = {
  children: React.PropTypes.func.isRequired,
}
```

The preceding component can be used in the following way:

```
<Name>
  {name => <div>Hello, {name}!</div>}
</Name>
```

The snippet renders `Hello, World!` again, but this time the name has been passed by the parent.

It should be clear how this pattern works, so let's look at the advantages of this approach.

The first benefit is that we can wrap components, passing them variables at runtime rather than fixed properties, as we do with HoCs.

A good example is a `Fetch` component that loads some data from an API endpoint and returns it down to the `children` function:

```
<Fetch url="...">
  {data => <List data={data} />}
</Fetch>
```

Secondly, composing components with this approach does not force the `children` to use some predefined prop names.

Since the function receives variables, their names can be decided by the developers who use the component.

That makes the Function as Child solution more flexible.

Last but not least, the wrapper is highly reusable because it does not make any assumptions about the children it receives, it just expects a function.

Due to this, the same Function as Child component can be used in different parts of the application, serving various children components.

Summary

In this chapter, we learned how to compose our reusable components and make them communicate effectively.

Props are the way to decouple the components from each other and create a clean and well-defined interface.

Then, we went through some of the most interesting composition patterns in React.

The first one was the so-called Container and Presentational pattern, which helps us separate the logic from the presentation and create more specialized components with a single responsibility.

We saw how React tried to solve the problem of sharing functionalities between components with mixins. Unfortunately, mixins solve those problems by adding several other ones, and they affect the maintainability of our applications.

One way to achieve the same goal without adding complexity is using HoCs, which are functions that take a component and return an enhanced one.

The recompose library provides some useful HoCs that can be used along with our custom ones so that our components have as little logic as possible in their implementation.

We learned how to deal with the context without needing to couple our components to it, thanks to HoCs.

Finally, we saw how we can compose components dynamically by following the Function as Child pattern.

It is now time to talk about data fetching and one-way data flow.

5
Proper Data Fetching

The goal of this chapter is to show the different data fetching patterns that we can put in place in a React application.

To find the best strategy, we have to clearly understand how the data flows within a tree of components in React.

It is important to know how the parent can communicate with its children and the other way around. It is also crucial to understand how unconnected siblings can share their data.

We will see some real-world examples of data fetching, transforming a base component into a well-structured one using HoCs.

Finally, we will see how existing libraries such as react-refetch can save us a lot of time by providing the core data fetching functionalities we need.

In this chapter, we will cover the following topics:

- The Unidirectional Data Flow of React and how it can make our applications easier to reason about
- How a child can communicate with its parent using callbacks
- The way two siblings can share data through their common parent
- How to create a generic HoC, which can fetch data from any API endpoints
- How react-refetch works and why it is a useful tool that we can integrate into our projects to make data fetching easier

Data flow

In the last two chapters, we saw how to create single reusable components and how to compose them together effectively.

Now, it is time learn how to build a proper data flow for sharing data across multiple components in our application.

React enforces a very interesting pattern to make data go from the root to the leaves. This pattern is usually called **Unidirectional Data Flow**, and we will see it in detail in this section.

As the name suggests, in React data flows in a single direction from the top to the bottom of the tree. This approach has many benefits because it simplifies the components' behavior and the relationship between components, making the code more predictable and maintainable.

Every component receives data from its parent in the form of props, and props cannot be modified. When the data is received, it can be transformed into new information and passed to the other children down the tree. Each of the children can hold a local state and use it as a prop for its nested components.

Up to this moment, we have only seen examples where the data is shared from parents to children components using props.

However, what happens if a child has to push data up to his parent? Or a parent has to be updated when its children's state changes? Also, what if two sibling components need to share data with each other? We will answer all these questions with a real-world example.

We will start with a simple component that has no children, and we will transform it into a cleaner and structured component step by step.

This approach will let us see the best pattern to apply in each phase in order to let the data flow across the tree.

Let's delve into the code creating a `Counter` component, which starts from 0 and has two buttons: one for incrementing the value and one for decrementing it.

We start by creating a class that extends the `Component` function from React:

```
class Counter extends React.Component
```

The class has a constructor where the counter is initialized to 0, and the event handlers are bound to the component itself:

```
constructor(props) {
  super(props)

  this.state = {
    counter: 0,
  }

  this.handleDecrement = this.handleDecrement.bind(this)
  this.handleIncrement = this.handleIncrement.bind(this)
}
```

The event handlers are simple, and they just change the state, adding or removing a unit from the current counter:

```
handleDecrement() {
  this.setState({
    counter: this.state.counter - 1,
  })
}

handleIncrement() {
  this.setState({
    counter: this.state.counter + 1,
  })
}
```

Finally, inside the render method, the current value is displayed, and the buttons with their onClick handlers are defined:

```
render() {
  return (
    <div>
      <h1>{this.state.counter}</h1>
      <button onClick={this.handleDecrement}>-</button>
      <button onClick={this.handleIncrement}>+</button>
    </div>
  )
}
```

Child-parent communication (callbacks)

There are no major issues with this component, apart from the fact that it does multiple things:

- It holds the counter value into the state
- It is responsible for showing the data
- It contains the logic for incrementing and decrementing the counter

It is always a good practice to split components into smaller ones, each with a very specific behavior, to improve the maintainability of the app and make it flexible when requirements change.

Consider that we need the same plus and minus buttons in another part of the application.

It would be great to reuse the buttons we defined inside the Counter, but the question is: If we move the buttons away from the component, how do we know when they get clicked on so that the counter can be updated?

In React, when we need to push information or simply trigger an event from children to the parent, we use **callbacks**.

Let's see how they work.

We create a Buttons component to display the increment and decrement buttons, which, instead of firing internal functions when they are clicked on, use the functions received from the props:

```
const Buttons = ({ onDecrement, onIncrement }) => (
  <div>
    <button onClick={onDecrement}>-</button>
    <button onClick={onIncrement}>+</button>
  </div>
)

Buttons.propTypes = {
  onDecrement: React.PropTypes.func,
  onIncrement: React.PropTypes.func,
}
```

It is a simple, stateless functional component where the onClick event handlers fire the functions received from the props.

Now it is time to see how to integrate this new component into the Counter.

We just replace the original markup with the component, passing the internal functions to the new child, as follows:

```
render() {
  return (
    <div>
      <h1>{this.state.counter}</h1>
      <Buttons
        onDecrement={this.handleDecrement}
        onIncrement={this.handleIncrement}
      />
    </div>
  )
}
```

Everything else remains the same, and the logic is still in the parent component.

The buttons are now dumb, and they are only able to notify their owner when they are clicked on.

So, every time we need the children to push data into the parent or simply inform the parent that something happened, we can pass callbacks and implement the rest of the logic inside the parent.

Common parent

Now, the `Counter` looks a bit better, and the `Buttons` are reusable. The last thing to be done to clean it up completely is to remove the display logic from it.

To do that, we can create a `Display` component that receives the value to display and just shows it on the screen:

```
const Display = ({ counter }) => <h1>{counter}</h1>

Display.propTypes = {
  counter: React.PropTypes.number,
}
```

Again, we can use a stateless functional component because there is no need to keep any state. As you may note here, splitting this component is not really needed because it just renders a h1 element. However, in your application, you may add CSS classes, display logic to change the color of the counter according to its value, and so on.

In general, our goal is to make components unaware of the data source so that we can reuse them with different sources in various parts of the application.

Using the new component in the `Counter` is easy, we just have to replace the old markup with the `Display` component, as follows:

```
render() {
  return (
    <div>
      <Display counter={this.state.counter} />
      <Buttons
        onDecrement={this.handleDecrement}
        onIncrement={this.handleIncrement}
      />
    </div>
  )
}
```

As you can see here, two sibling components are communicating through their common parent.

When the `Buttons` get clicked on, they notify the parent, which sends the updated value to the `Display` component. This is a very common pattern in React, and it is an effective solution to share data across components that do not have a direct relation.

The data always flows from parents to children, but children can notify the parent and make the tree re-render with the new information.

Every time we need to make two unrelated components communicate, we have to find the common parent between them and keep the state at that level so that, when the state is updated, both components receive fresh data from the props.

Data fetching

In the preceding section, we saw the different patterns we can put in place to share data between components in the tree.

It is now time to view how to fetch data in React and where the data fetching logic should be located.

The examples in this section use the fetch function to make web requests, which is a modern replacement for XMLHttpRequest.

At the time of writing, it is natively implemented in Chrome and FireFox and if you need to support different browsers, you must use the fetch **polyfill** by GitHub:

```
https://github.com/github/fetch
```

We are also going to use the public GitHub APIs to load some data and the endpoint we will use is the one that returns a list of **gists**, given a username:

```
https://api.github.com/users/:username/gists
```

Gists are snippets of code that can be easily shared between developers.

The first component that we will build is a simple list of the gists created by the user, called *gaearon* (*Dan Abramov*).

Let's delve into some code and create a class.

We use a class because we need to store an internal state and use the life cycle methods:

```
class Gists extends React.Component
```

Then, we define a `constructor`, where we initialize the state:

```
constructor(props) {
  super(props)

  this.state = { gists: [] }
}
```

Now comes the interesting part: data fetching.

There are two lifecycle hooks where we can put the data fetching: `componentWillMount` and `componentDidMount`.

The first is fired before the component gets rendered for the first time and the second is fired right after the component is mounted.

Using the first seems to be the right because we want to load the data as soon as we can, but there is a caveat.

The `componentWillMount` function, in fact, is fired on both server and client-side rendering.

We will see the server-side rendering in detail in Chapter 8, *Server-Side Rendering for Fun and Profit*, but, for now, you just need to know that firing an async API call when the component gets rendered on the server can give you unexpected results.

We will then use the `componentDidMount` hook so that we can be sure that the API endpoint is called on the browser only.

This also means that, during the first render, the list of gists is empty and we might want to show a spinner by applying one of the techniques that we saw in Chapter 2, *Clean Up Your Code*, which is beyond the scope of the current section.

As we said before, we are going to use the fetch function and hit the GitHub APIs to retrieve gaearon's gists:

```
componentDidMount() {
  fetch('https://api.github.com/users/gaearon/gists')
    .then(response => response.json())
    .then(gists => this.setState({ gists }))
}
```

This code needs a little bit of explanation. When the `componentDidMount` hook gets fired, we call the fetch function against the GitHub APIs.

The fetch function returns a `Promise` and, when it gets resolved, we receive a response object with a JSON function that returns the JSON content of the response itself.

When the JSON is parsed and returned, we can save the raw gists inside the internal state of the component to make them available in the render method:

```
render() {
  return (
    <ul>
      {this.state.gists.map(gist => (
        <li key={gist.id}>{gist.description}</li>
      ))}
    </ul>
  )
}
```

The render method is simple–we just loop through the gists and map each one of them into a `<li>` element that shows their description.

You might have noted the key attribute of `<li>`. We use it for performance reasons that you will understand by the end of the book.

If you try to remove the attribute, you will get a warning from React inside the browser's console.

The component works and everything is fine, but as we learned in the previous sections, we could, for example, separate the rendering logic into a subcomponent to make it more simple and testable.

Moving the component away is not a problem because we have seen how components in different parts of the application can receive the data they need from their parents.

Now, it is very common to have the need to fetch data from the APIs in different parts of the codebase, and we do not want to duplicate the code.

A solution we can apply to remove the data logic from the component and reuse it across the application is by creating a HoC.

In this case, the HoC would load the data on behalf of the enhanced component and it would provide the data to the child in the form of props.

Let's see what it looks like.

As we know, an HoC is a function that accepts a component and some parameters and returns a new component that has some special behaviors attached to it.

We are going to use the partial application to receive the parameters first, and then the actual component as the second parameter:

```
const withData = url => Component => (...)
```

We have called the `withData` function following the `with*` pattern.

The function accepts the URL from which the data has to be loaded and the component that needs the data to work.

The implementation is pretty similar to the component in the preceding example apart from the fact that the URL is now a parameter and, inside the render method, we use the child component.

The function returns a class defined as follows:

```
class extends React.Component
```

It has a constructor to set the initial empty state.

Note that the property we use to store the data is now called data because we are building a generic component and we do not want it to be tied to a particular object shape or collection:

```
constructor(props) {
  super(props)

  this.state = { data: [] }
}
```

Inside the `componentDidMount` hook, the fetch function is fired and the data returned from the server is converted to JSON and stored into the state:

```
componentDidMount() {
  fetch(url)
    .then(response => response.json())
    .then(data => this.setState({ data }))
}
```

It is important to note that now the URL is set using the first parameter received from the HoC.

In this way, we can reuse it to make any API call to any endpoint.

Finally, we render the given component spreading the props because we want our HoC to be transparent.

We spread the state as well to pass the JSON data to the child component:

```
render() {
  return <Component {...this.props} {...this.state} />
}
```

Great, the HoC is ready.

We can now wrap any components of our application and provide data to them from any URL.

Let's see how to use it.

First of all, we have to create a dumb component that receives the data and displays it, using the markup of the initial example:

```
const List = ({ data: gists }) => (
  <ul>
    {gists.map(gist => (
      <li key={gist.id}>{gist.description}</li>
```

```
    )))}
  </ul>
)

List.propTypes = {
  data: React.PropTypes.array,
}
```

We have used a stateless functional component because we do not need to store any state nor define handlers inside it, which is usually a big win.

The prop containing the response from the API is called `data`, which is generic and not useful, but we can easily rename it, thanks to ES2015, and give it a more meaningful name.

It is now time to see how to use our `withData` HoC and make it pass the data down to the `List` component we just created.

Thanks to the partial application, we can first specialize the HoC to make a specific call and use it many times, as follows:

```
const withGists = withData(
  'https://api.github.com/users/gaearon/gists'
)
```

This is great because we can now wrap any component with the new `withGists` function and it will receive gaeron's gists without specifying the URL multiple times.

Finally, we wrap the component and get a new one:

```
const ListWithGists = withGists(List)
```

We can now put the enhanced component anywhere within our application, and it just works.

Our `withData` HoC is great, but it is only able to load static URLs, while in the real world URLs often depend on parameters or props.

Unfortunately, the props are unknown at the moment we apply the HoC, so we need a hook that is called when the props are available and before making the API call.

What we can do is change the HoC to accept two types of URLs: a string, as we have done until now, and a function, which receives the component's props and returns a URL that depends on the received parameters.

That is pretty straightforward to do; we just have to change the `componentDidMount` hook, as follows:

```
componentDidMount() {
  const endpoint = typeof url === 'function'
    ? url(this.props)
    : url

  fetch(endpoint)
    .then(response => response.json())
    .then(data => this.setState({ data }))
}
```

If the URL is a function, we fire it by passing the props as parameters, while if it is a string we use it directly.

We can now use the HoC in the following way:

```
const withGists = withData(
  props => `https://api.github.com/users/${props.username}/gists`
)
```

Where the username for loading the gists can be set in the props of the component:

```
<ListWithGists username="gaearon" />
```

React-refetch

Now, our HoC works as expected and we can reuse it across the code base without any problems.

The question is, What should we do if we need more features?

For example, we may want to post some data to the server or fetch the data again when the props change.

Also, we may not want to load the data on `componentDidMount` and apply some lazy loading patterns instead.

We could obviously write all the features we need, but there is an existing library that has a lot of useful functionalities, and it is ready to be used.

The library is called react-refetch, and it is maintained by developers from *Heroku*.

Let's see how we can use it effectively to replace our HoC.

From the previous section, we have a `List` component, which is a stateless functional component that can receive a collection of gists; it displays the description for each one of them:

```
const List = ({ data: gists }) => (
  <ul>
    {gists.map(gist => (
      <li key={gist.id}>{gist.description}</li>
    ))}
  </ul>
)

List.propTypes = {
  data: React.PropTypes.array,
}
```

By wrapping this component inside the `withData` HoC, we are able to provide data to it in a transparent way through props. We just have to enhance it, passing the URL of the endpoint.

With react-refetch, we can do the same thing; so, first of all, we install the library:

npm install react-refetch --save

Then, we import the connect function inside our module:

```
import { connect } from 'react-refetch'
```

Finally, we decorate our component using the `connect` HoC.

We use the partial application technique to specialize the function and reuse it:

```
const connectWithGists = connect(({ username }) => ({
  gists: `https://api.github.com/users/${username}/gists`,
}))
```

The preceding code needs a bit of explanation.

We use the `connect` function, passing a function to it as a parameter. The parameter function receives the props (and the context) as parameters so that we can create dynamic URLs based on the current properties of the component.

Our callback function returns an object where the keys are the identifiers of the request, and the values are the URLs.

The URL is not limited to being a string; we'll see later how we can add multiple parameters to the request.

At this point, we enhance our component with the function we just created, as follows:

```
const ListWithGists = connectWithGists(List)
```

We now have to make small changes to the initial component to make it work well with the new HoC.

First of all, the parameter is not called `data` anymore; it is called `gists`.

In fact, react-refetch will inject a property with the same name of the key that we specified in the connect function.

The `gists` prop is not the actual data, but it is a particular type of object, called `PromiseState`.

A `PromiseState` object is a synchronous representation of a `Promise` and it has some useful attributes such as pending or fulfilled, which we can use to show a spinner or a list of data.

There is also a rejected property that we can use in case of errors.

When the request is fulfilled, we can access the data we wanted to load using the `value` property and loop through it to display the gists:

```
const List = ({ gists }) => (
  gists.fulfilled && (
    <ul>
      {gists.value.map(gist => (
        <li key={gist.id}>{gist.description}</li>
      ))}
    </ul>
  )
)
```

As soon as the stateless functional component gets rendered, we do a check to validate if the request is fulfilled; if it is, we show the list using the `gists.value` property.

Everything else remains the same.

We also have to update the `propTypes` and change the name of the received prop and its type:

```
List.propTypes = {
  gists: React.PropTypes.object,
}
```

Now that we have this library in our project, we can add more functionalities to our `List` component.

For example, we can add a button to start the gists.

Let's start with the UI and then add the real API call, thanks to react-refetch.

We do not want to add too many responsibilities to the `List` component as its role is to display the list; so, we change it to use a subcomponent for each row.

We call the new component `Gist`, and we are going to use it inside the loop in the following way:

```
const List = ({ gists }) => (
  gists.fulfilled && (
    <ul>
      {gists.value.map(gist => (
        <Gist key={gist.id} {...gist} />
      ))}
    </ul>
  )
)
```

We just replaced the `<li>` element with the `Gist` component, and we spread the gist object to it so that it receives single properties and becomes easier to test and maintain.

The `Gist` component is a stateless functional component because the starring logic is handled by react-refetch and we do not need any state or event handlers.

The component receives the description and, for now, the only difference from the previous markup is that it has a +1 button, to which we will add some functionalities soon:

```
const Gist = ({ description }) => (
  <li>
    {description}
    <button>+1</button>
  </li>
)

Gist.propTypes = {
```

```
    description: React.PropTypes.string,
}
```

The URL of the endpoint to star a gist is the following:

```
https://api.github.com/gists/:id/star?access_token=:access_token
```

Here, `:id` is the id of the gist that we want to star, and the access token is the authentication token required to run the action.

There are different ways of getting an access token, and they are well explained in the GitHub documentation.

They are also outside the scope of this book, so we are not going to cover them in this section.

The next step is adding a function to the `onClick` event of the button to make the API call with the ID of the gist.

The connect function of react-refetch accepts a function as the first argument and the function has to return an object of requests, as we have previously seen.

If the values of the requests are strings, then the data is fetched as soon as the props are available.

If the value of a request key is a function instead, it gets passed into the component, and it can be fired lazily.

For example, it can be triggered when a particular event occurs.

Let's delve into the code:

```
const token = 'access_token=123'

const connectWithStar = connect(({ id }) => ({
  star: () => ({
    starResponse: {
      url: `https://api.github.com/gists/${id}/star?${token}`,
      method: 'PUT',
    },
  }),
}))
```

First, we partially apply the collection function, and we use the `id` prop to compose the URL.

We then define an object of requests, where the key is `star`, and the value is a function that, again, returns an object of requests. In this case, the value of the key `starResponse` is not a simple string, but an object with two parameters: URL and method.

This is because, by default, the library fires an HTTP GET, but in this case we are required to use a PUT to star a gist.

It is now time to enhance our component:

```
const GistWithStar = connectWithStar(Gist)
```

Also, it is time to use the `star` function inside it to fire the request:

```
const Gist = ({ description, star }) => (
  <li>
    {description}
    <button onClick={star}>+1</button>
  </li>
)

Gist.propTypes = {
  description: React.PropTypes.string,
  star: React.PropTypes.func,
}
```

As you can see, it is very simple; the component receives the star function, where star is the name of the request that we defined in the connect function. The function gets fired when the button is clicked on.

This is the final result in the browser window:

You may have noted that, thanks to react-refetch, we can keep our components stateless and unaware of the actions that they are firing.

This makes tests easier, and also we can change the implementation of the HoC without modifying the subcomponent.

Summary

The journey through data fetching in React has come to an end and now you know how to send and retreive data to and from API endpoints.

We saw how data flow works in React and why the approach it enforces can make our applications simple and clean.

We went through some of the most common patterns to make child and parent communicate using callbacks.

We learned how we can use a common parent to share data across components that are not directly connected.

In the second section, we started with a simple component, which was able to load data from GitHub, and we made it reusable, thanks to HoC.

We have now mastered the techniques that let us abstract the logic away from components so that we can make them as dumb as possible, improving their testability.

Finally, we learned how we can use react-refetch to apply data fetching patterns to our components and avoid reinventing the wheel.

In the next chapter, we will see how to work with React effectively in the browser.

6
Write Code for the Browser

There are some specific operations we can do when we work with React and the browser. For example, we can ask our users to enter some information using forms, and we will look at how, in React, we can apply different techniques to deal with them.

We can implement **Uncontrolled Components** and let the fields keep their internal states, or we can use Controlled ones, where we have full control over the state of the fields.

In this chapter, we will also look at how events in React work and how the library implements some advanced techniques to give us a consistent interface across different browsers. We will also look at some interesting solutions that the React team has implemented to make the event system very performant.

After the events, we will jump into refs to look at how we can access the underlying DOM nodes in our React components. This represents a powerful feature, but it should be used carefully because it breaks some of the conventions that make React easy to work with.

After the refs, we will look at how we can easily implement animations with the React add-ons and third-party libraries such as **react-motion**. Finally, we will learn how easy it is to work with SVGs in React, and how we can create dynamically configurable icons for our applications.

In this chapter, we will go through the following:

- Using different techniques to create forms with React
- Listening to DOM events and implementing custom handlers
- A way of performing imperative operations on DOM nodes using refs
- Creating simple animations that work across the different browsers
- The React way of generating SVGs

Forms

As soon as we start building a real application with React, we need to interact with the users. If we want to ask for information from our users within the browser, forms are the most common solution. Due to the way the library works and its declarative nature, dealing with input fields and other form elements is non-trivial with React, but as soon as we understand its logic, it becomes clear.

Uncontrolled components

Let's start with a basic example: displaying a form with an input field and a submit button.

The code is pretty straightforward:

```
const Uncontrolled = () => (
  <form>
    <input type="text" />
    <button>Submit</button>
  </form>
)
```

If we run the preceding snippet in the browser, we can see exactly what we expect: an input field in which we can write something, and a clickable button. This is an example of an Uncontrolled Component, where we do not set the value of the input field, but we let the component manage its internal state.

Most likely, we want to do something with the value of the element when the submit button is clicked.

For example, we may want to send the data to an API endpoint.

We can do this easily by adding an `onChange` listener (we will talk more about event listeners later in this chapter).

Let's look at what it means to add a listener.

First, we have to change the component from stateless to a class because we need to define some functions and a state:

```
class Uncontrolled extends React.Component
```

The class has a constructor where we bind the event listener:

```
constructor(props) {
  super(props)

  this.handleChange = this.handleChange.bind(this)
}
```

Then we define the event listener itself:

```
handleChange({ target }) {
  console.log(target.value)
}
```

The event listener is receiving an event object, where the target represents the field that generated the event, and we are interested in its value. We start by just logging it, because it is important to proceed with small steps, but we will store the value into the state soon.

Finally, we render the form:

```
render() {
  return (
    <form>
      <input type="text" onChange={this.handleChange} />
      <button>Submit</button>
    </form>
  )
}
```

If we render the component inside the browser and type the word **React** into the form field, we will see something like the following inside the console:

```
R
Re
Rea
Reac
React
```

The `handleChange` listener is fired every time the value of the input changes. Therefore, our function is called once for each typed character. The next step is to store the value entered by the user and make it available when the user clicks the submit button.

We just have to change the implementation of the handler to store into the state instead of logging it, as follows:

```
handleChange({ target }) {
  this.setState({
    value: target.value,
  })
}
```

Getting notified of when the form is submitted is very similar to listening to the change event of the input field; they are both events called by the browser when something happens.

So, we add a second event handler inside the constructor, as follows:

```
constructor(props) {
  super(props)

  this.state = {
    value: '',
  }

  this.handleChange = this.handleChange.bind(this)
  this.handleSubmit = this.handleSubmit.bind(this)
}
```

We may also want to initialize the value property of the state as an empty string, in case the button gets clicked before any change event is triggered.

Let's define the `handleSubmit` function where we just log the value. In a real-world scenario you could send the data to an API endpoint or pass it to another component.

```
handleSubmit(e) {
  e.preventDefault()

  console.log(this.state.value)
}
```

This handler is pretty straightforward: we just log the value currently stored in the state. We also want to prevent the default behavior of the browser when the form is submitted, to perform a custom action.

This seems reasonable, and it works very well for a single field. The question now is, what if we have multiple fields? Suppose we have tens of different fields?

Let's start with a basic example, where we create each field and handler manually, and look at how we can improve it by applying different levels of optimization.

Let's create a new form with first and last name fields. We can reuse the Uncontrolled class we just created and change the constructor as follows:

```
constructor(props) {
  super(props)

  this.state = {
    firstName: '',
    lastName: '',
  }

  this.handleChangeFirstName =
    this.handleChangeFirstName.bind(this)
  this.handleChangeLastName = this.handleChangeLastName.bind(this)
  this.handleSubmit = this.handleSubmit.bind(this)
}
```

We initialize the two fields inside the state and we define an event handler for each one of the fields as well. As you may notice, this does not scale very well when there are lots of fields, but it is important to clearly understand the problem before moving to a more flexible solution.

Now, we implement the new handlers:

```
handleChangeFirstName({ target }) {
  this.setState({
    firstName: target.value,
  })
}

handleChangeLastName({ target }) {
  this.setState({
    lastName: target.value,
  })
}
```

We also have to change the submit handler a little bit so that it displays first and last name when it gets clicked:

```
handleSubmit(e) {
  e.preventDefault()

  console.log(`${this.state.firstName} ${this.state.lastName}`)
}
```

Finally, we describe our elements structure inside the `render` method:

```
render() {
  return (
    <form onSubmit={this.handleSubmit}>
      <input type="text" onChange={this.handleChangeFirstName} />
      <input type="text" onChange={this.handleChangeLastName} />
      <button>Submit</button>
    </form>
  )
}
```

We are ready to go: if we run the preceding component in the browser we will see two fields, and if we type **Dan** into the first one and **Abramov** into the second one we will see the full name displayed in the browser console when the form is submitted.

Again, this works fine, and we can do some interesting things in this way, but it does not handle complex scenarios without requiring us to write a lot of boilerplate code.

Let's look at how we can optimize it a little bit.

Our goal is basically to use a single change handler so that we can add an arbitrary number of fields without creating new listeners.

Let's go back to the constructor and define a single change handler:

```
constructor(props) {
  super(props)

  this.state = {
    firstName: '',
    lastName: '',
  }

  this.handleChange = this.handleChange.bind(this)
  this.handleSubmit = this.handleSubmit.bind(this)
}
```

We may still want to initialize the values, and later in this section we will look at how to provide pre-filled values to the form.

Now, the interesting bit is the way we can modify the onChange handler implementation to make it work with different fields:

```
handleChange({ target }) {
  this.setState({
    [target.name]: target.value,
  })
}
```

As we have seen previously, the target property of the event we receive represents the input field that has fired the event, so we can use the name of the field and its value as variables.

We then have to set the name for each field, and we are going to do it in the render method:

```
render() {
  return (
    <form onSubmit={this.handleSubmit}>
      <input
        type="text"
        name="firstName"
        onChange={this.handleChange}
      />
      <input
        type="text"
        name="lastName"
        onChange={this.handleChange}
      />
      <button>Submit</button>
    </form>
  )
}
```

That's it; we can now add as many fields as we want without creating additional handlers.

Controlled components

The next thing we are going to look at is how we can pre-fill the form fields with some values, which we may receive from the server or as props from the parent.

To fully understand the concept, we will start again from a very simple stateless function component, and we will improve it step by step.

The first example shows a predefined value inside the input field:

```
const Controlled = () => (
  <form>
    <input type="text" value="Hello React" />
    <button>Submit</button>
  </form>
)
```

If we run this component inside the browser, we realize that it shows the default value as expected, but it does not let us change the value or type anything else inside it.

The reason it does that is because, in React, we declare what we want to see on the screen, and setting a fixed value attribute ends up always rendering that value, no matter what other actions are taken. This is unlikely to be a behavior we want in a real-world application.

If we open the console, React itself is telling us that we are doing something wrong:

```
You provided a `value` prop to a form field without an `onChange`
handler. This will render a read-only field.
```

And that is exactly what happened.

Now, if we just want the input field to have a default value and then be able to change it by typing, we can use the `defaultValue` property:

```
const Controlled = () => (
  <form>
    <input type="text" defaultValue="Hello React" />
    <button>Submit</button>
  </form>
)
```

In this way, the field is going to show `Hello React` when it is rendered, but then the user can type anything inside it and change its value. This is OK, and it works, but we want to fully control the value of the component and to do so, we should transform the component from a stateless functional one to a class:

```
class Controlled extends React.Component
```

As usual, we start defining a constructor where we initialize the state, this time with the default values of the fields. We also bind the event handlers we need to make the form work.

We will use a single handler, which will update the state using the name attribute, as we have seen in the optimized version of the Uncontrolled Components example:

```
constructor(props) {
  super(props)

  this.state = {
    firstName: 'Dan',
    lastName: 'Abramov',
  }

  this.handleChange = this.handleChange.bind(this)
  this.handleSubmit = this.handleSubmit.bind(this)
}
```

The handlers are the same as the previous ones:

```
handleChange({ target }) {
  this.setState({
    [target.name]: target.value,
  })
}

handleSubmit(e) {
  e.preventDefault()

  console.log(`${this.state.firstName} ${this.state.lastName}`)
}
```

The important thing to change is inside the render method. In fact, we will use the value attributes of the input fields to set their initial values as well as the updated one:

```
render() {
  return (
    <form onSubmit={this.handleSubmit}>
      <input
        type="text"
        name="firstName"
        value={this.state.firstName}
        onChange={this.handleChange}
      />
      <input
        type="text"
        name="lastName"
        value={this.state.lastName}
        onChange={this.handleChange}
      />
      <button>Submit</button>
```

```
        </form>
    )
}
```

The first time the form is rendered, React uses the initial values from the state as the value of the input fields. When the user types something in the field, the `handleChange` function is called and the new value for the field is stored into the state.

When the state changes, React re-renders the component and uses it again to reflect the current value of the input fields.

We now have full control over the value of the fields, and we call this pattern **Controlled Components**.

JSON schema

Now that we know how the forms work in React, we can move into something that helps us automate the form creation, avoid writing a lot of boilerplate, and keep our code much cleaner.

A popular solution is the `react-jsonschema-form`, maintained by mozilla-services, and the first thing we must do is install it using `npm`:

```
npm install --save react-jsonschema-form
```

Once the library is installed, we import it inside our component:

```
import Form from 'react-jsonschema-form'
```

And we define a schema as follows:

```
const schema = {
  type: 'object',
  properties: {
    firstName: { type: 'string', default: 'Dan' },
    lastName: { type: 'string', default: 'Abramov' },
  },
}
```

We will not go into the details of the JSON Schema format in this book: the important bit here is that we can describe the fields of our forms using a configuration object instead of creating multiple HTML elements.

As you can see in the example, we set the type of the schema to object and then we declare the properties of the form, `firstName` and `lastName`, each one with a string type and its default value.

If we then pass the schema to the `Form` component we imported from the library, a form will be generated for us automatically.

Once more, let's start with a simple stateless functional component so that we can add features to it iteratively:

```
const JSONSchemaForm = () => (
  <Form schema={schema} />
)
```

Now, if we render this component inside the page, we will see a form with the fields we declared in the schema and a submit button.

We now want to be notified when the form is submitted, to do something with the form data.

The first thing we have to do to create an event handler is transform the stateless functional component into a class:

```
class JSONSchemaForm extends React.Component
```

Inside the constructor, we bind the event handler:

```
constructor(props) {
  super(props)

  this.handleSubmit = this.handleSubmit.bind(this)
}
```

In the preceding example, we just log the form data into the console, but in a real-world application you may want to post the fields to an endpoint.

The `handleSubmit` handler is receiving an object, which has a `formData` attribute that contains the names and the values of the form fields:

```
handleSubmit({ formData }) {
  console.log(formData)
}
```

Finally, our render method looks as follows:

```
render() {
  return (
    <Form schema={schema} onSubmit={this.handleSubmit} />
  )
}
```

Here, the schema prop is the schema object we previously defined. It can be defined statically, as in the current example, or it can be received from the server or composed using props.

We just attach our handler to the `onSubmit` callback of the `Form` component provided by the library and we have created a working form easily.

There are also different callbacks, such as `onChange`, which is fired every time the value of a field changes, and `onError`, which is fired whenever the form is submitted using invalid data.

Events

Events work in a slightly different way across the various browsers. React tries to abstract the way events work and give developers a consistent interface to deal with. This is a great feature of React, because we can forget about the browsers we are targeting and write event handlers and functions that are vendor-agnostic.

To offer this feature, React introduces the concept of the **Synthetic Event**. A Synthetic Event is an object that wraps the original event object provided by the browser, and it has the same properties, no matter the browser where it is created.

To attach an event listener to a node and get the event object when the event is fired, we can use a simple convention which recalls the way events are attached to the DOM nodes. In fact, we can use the word *on* plus the camelCased event name (for example, `onKeyDown`) to define the callback to be fired when the events happen. A popular convention is to name the event handler functions after the event name and prefix them using *handle* (for example, `handleKeyDown`).

We have seen this pattern in action in the previous examples, where we were listening to the `onChange` event of the form fields.

Let's reiterate a basic event-listener example to see how we can organize multiple events inside the same component in a nicer way.

We are going to implement a simple button, and we start, as usual, by creating a class:

```
class Button extends React.Component
```

We add a constructor where we bind the event listener:

```
constructor(props) {
  super(props)

  this.handleClick = this.handleClick.bind(this)
}
```

We define the event handler itself:

```
handleClick(syntheticEvent) {
  console.log(syntheticEvent instanceof MouseEvent)
  console.log(syntheticEvent.nativeEvent instanceof MouseEvent)
}
```

As you can see here, we are doing a very simple thing: we just check the type of the event object we receive from React and the type of the native event attached to it. We expect the first to return `false` and the second to return `true`.

You should never need to access the original native event, but it is good to know you can do it if you need to. Finally, in the render method, we define the button with the `onClick` attribute to which we attach our event listener:

```
render() {
  return (
    <button onClick={this.handleClick}>Click me!</button>
  )
}
```

Now, suppose we want to attach a second handler to the button which listens to the double click event. One solution would be to create a new separate handler and attach it to the button using the `onDoubleClick` attribute, as follows:

```
<button
  onClick={this.handleClick}
  onDoubleClick={this.handleDoubleClick}
>
  Click me!
</button>
```

Remember that we always aim to write less boilerplate and avoid duplicating the code. For that reason, a common practice is to write a **single event handler** for each component, which can trigger different actions according to the event type.

This technique is described in a collection of patterns by Michael Chan:

```
http://reactpatterns.com/#event-switch
```

First, we change the constructor of the component, because we now want it to bind the new generic event handler:

```
constructor(props) {
  super(props)

  this.handleEvent = this.handleEvent.bind(this)
}
```

Second, we implement the generic event handler:

```
handleEvent(event) {
  switch (event.type) {
    case 'click':
      console.log('clicked')
      break

    case 'dblclick':
      console.log('double clicked')
      break

    default:
      console.log('unhandled', event.type)
  }
}
```

The generic event handler receives the event object and switches on the event type in order to fire the right action. This is particularly useful if we want to call a function on each event (for example, analytics) or if some events share the same logic.

Finally, we attach the new event listener to the onClick and onDoubleClick attributes:

```
render() {
  return (
    <button
      onClick={this.handleEvent}
      onDoubleClick={this.handleEvent}
    >
      Click me!
    </button>
```

```
    )
  }
```

From this point on, whenever we need to create a new event handler for the same component, instead of creating a new method and binding it, we can just add a new case to the switch.

A couple more interesting things to know about events in React are that Synthetic Events are reused, and that there is a **single global handler**. The first concept means that we cannot store a synthetic event and reuse it later because it becomes null right after the action. This technique is very good in terms of performance, but it can be problematic if we want to store the event inside the state of the component for some reason. To solve the problem, React gives us a `persist` method on the Synthetic Events, which we can call to make the event persistent so that we can store it and retrieve it later.

The second very interesting implementation detail is again about performance, and it regards the way React attaches the event handlers to the DOM.

Whenever we use the on* attributes, we are describing to React the behavior we want to achieve, but the library does not attach the actual event handler to the underlying DOM nodes.

What it does instead is attach a single event handler to the root element, which listens to all the events, thanks to the **event bubbling**. When an event we are interested in is fired by the browser, React calls the handler on the specific components on its behalf. This technique is called **event delegation** and is used for memory and speed optimization.

Refs

One of the reasons people love React is because it is declarative. Being declarative means that you just describe what you want to be displayed on the screen at any given point in time and React takes care of the communications with the browser. This feature makes React very easy to reason about and it is very powerful at the same time.

However, there might be some cases where you need to access the underlying DOM nodes to perform some imperative operations. It should be avoided because, in most cases, there is a more React-compliant solution to achieve the same result, but it is important to know that we have the possibility to do it and to know how it works so that we can make the right decision.

Suppose we want to create a simple form with an input element and a button, and we want it to behave in such a way that when the button is clicked, the input field gets focused.

What we want to do basically is to call the `focus` method on the input node, the actual DOM instance of the input, inside the browser's window.

Let's create a class called `Focus` with a constructor where we bind the `handleClick` method:

```
class Focus extends React.Component
```

We will listen to the click events on the button to focus the input field:

```
constructor(props) {
  super(props)

  this.handleClick = this.handleClick.bind(this)
}
```

Then we implement the actual `handleClick` method:

```
handleClick() {
  this.element.focus()
}
```

As you can see, we are referencing the element attribute of the class and calling the focus method on it.

To understand where it comes from, you just have to check the implementation of the render method:

```
render() {
  return (
    <form>
      <input
        type="text"
        ref={element => (this.element = element)}
      />
      <button onClick={this.handleClick}>Focus</button>
    </form>
  )
}
```

Here comes the core of the logic. We create a form with an input element inside it and we define a function on its ref attribute.

The callback we defined is called when the component gets mounted, and the element parameter represents the DOM instance of the input. It is important to know that, when the component gets unmounted, the same callback is called with a `null` parameter, to free the memory. What we are doing in the callback is storing the reference of the element to be able to use it in the future (for example, when the `handleClick` method is fired). Then we have the button with its event handler. Running the preceding code in a browser will show the form with the field and the button, and clicking on the button will focus the input field, as expected.

 As mentioned previously, in general, we should try to avoid using refs because they force the code to be more imperative, and harder to read and maintain.

The scenarios where we might need to use it without any other solutions are the ones where we are integrating our components with other imperative libraries, such as jQuery.

It is important to know that when setting the ref callback on a non-native component (a custom component that starts with an uppercase letter), the reference we receive as a parameter of the callback is not a DOM node instance, but the instance of the component itself. This is really powerful, because it gives us access to the internal instance of a child component, but it is also dangerous and should be avoided.

To see an example of this solution, we are going to create two components:

- The first one is a simple controlled input field, which exposes a reset function that resets the value of the input itself to an empty string
- The second component is a form with the previous input field, and a reset button which fires the instance method when clicked

Let's start by creating the input:

```
class Input extends React.Component
```

We define a constructor with a default state (empty string), and bind the `onChange` method we need to control the component, and the `reset` method, which represents the public API of the component:

```
constructor(props) {
  super(props)

  this.state = {
    value: '',
  }
```

```
      this.reset = this.reset.bind(this)
      this.handleChange = this.handleChange.bind(this)
   }
```

The `reset` function is very simple, and just brings the state back to empty:

```
reset() {
   this.setState({
      value: '',
   })
}
```

The `handleChange` is pretty simple as well, and it just keeps the state of the component in sync with the current value of the input element:

```
handleChange({ target }) {
   this.setState({
      value: target.value,
   })
}
```

Finally, inside the `render` method, we define our `input` field with its controlled value and the event handler:

```
render() {
   return (
      <input
         type="text"
         value={this.state.value}
         onChange={this.handleChange}
      />
   )
}
```

Now we are going to create the `Reset` component, which uses the preceding component, and call its `reset` method when the button is clicked:

```
class Reset extends React.Component
```

Inside the constructor, we bind the event handler, as usual:

```
constructor(props) {
   super(props)

   this.handleClick = this.handleClick.bind(this)
}
```

The interesting part is the code inside the `handleClick` function, because this is where we can call the `reset` method on the instance of the input:

```
handleClick() {
  this.element.reset()
}
```

Finally, we define our `render` method as follows:

```
render() {
  return (
    <form>
      <Input ref={element => (this.element = element)} />
      <button onClick={this.handleClick}>Reset</button>
    </form>
  )
}
```

As you can see here, referencing node elements or instances is basically the same in terms of ref callback.

This is pretty powerful, because we can easily access methods on the components, but we should be careful, because it breaks the encapsulation and makes refactoring pretty hard. Suppose, in fact, that you need to rename the `reset` function for some reason; you have to check all the parent components that are using it and change them as well.

React is great because it gives us a declarative API to use in all cases, but we can also access the underlying DOM nodes and components instances in case we need them to create more advanced interactions and complex structures.

Animations

When we think about UIs and the browser, we must surely think about animations as well.

Animated UIs are more pleasant for users, and they are a very important tool to show users that something has happened or is about to occur.

This section does not aim to be an exhaustive guide to creating animations and beautiful UIs; the goal here is to provide you some basic information about the common solutions we can put in place to animate our React components.

For a UI library such as React, it is crucial to provide an easy way for developers to create and manage animations. React comes with an add-on, called `react-addons-css-transition-group`, which is a component that helps us build animations in a declarative way. Again, being able to perform operations declaratively is incredibly powerful, and it makes the code much easier to reason about and share with the team.

Let's look at how to apply a simple fade-in effect to a text with the React add-on, and then we will perform the same operation using `react-motion`, a third-party library that makes creating complex animations even easier.

The first thing to do to start building an animated component is to install the add-on:

```
npm install --save react-addons-css-transition-group
```

Once we have done that, we can import the component:

```
import CSSTransitionGroup from 'react-addons-css-transition-group'
```

Then we just wrap the component to which we want to apply the animation with it:

```
const Transition = () => (
  <CSSTransitionGroup
    transitionName="fade"
    transitionAppear
    transitionAppearTimeout={500}
  >
    <h1>Hello React</h1>
  </CSSTransitionGroup>
)
```

As you can see, there are some props that need explanation.

First, we are declaring a `transitionName`. The `ReactCSSTransitionGroup` applies a class with the name of that property to the child element so that we can then use CSS transitions to create our animations.

With a single class, we cannot easily create a proper animation, and that is why the transition group applies multiple classes according to the state of the animation.

In this case, with the `transitionAppear` prop, we are telling the component that we want to animate the children when they appear on the screen.

So, what the library does is apply the `fade-appear` class (where fade is the value of the `transitionName` prop) to the component as soon as it gets rendered.

On the next tick, the class `fade-appear-active` is applied so that we can fire our animation from the initial state to the new one, using CSS.

We also have to set the `transitionAppearTimeout` property to tell React the length of the animation so it does not remove elements from the DOM before animations are completed.

The CSS to make an element fade in is as follows.

First we define the opacity of the element in the initial state:

```
.fade-appear {
  opacity: 0.01;
}
```

Then we define our transition using the second class, which starts as soon as it gets applied to the element:

```
.fade-appear.fade-appear-active {
  opacity: 1;
  transition: opacity .5s ease-in;
}
```

We are transitioning the opacity from `0.01` to `1` in `500ms` using the ease-in function.

That is pretty easy, but we can create more complex animations, and we can also animate different states of the component.

For example, the `*-enter` and `*-enter-active` classes are applied when a new element is added as a child of the transition group.

A similar thing applies to removing elements.

React motion

As soon as the complexity of the animations grows, or when we need animations that depend on other animations, or, which is more advanced, when we need to apply some physics-based behavior to our components, we realize that the transition group is not helping us enough, so we may consider using a third-party library.

The most popular library to create animations in React is `react-motion`, maintained by Cheng Lou. It provides a very clean and easy API that gives us a very powerful tool to create any animations.

To use it, we first have to install it:

```
npm install --save react-motion
```

Once the installation is successfully completed, we import the **motion** component and the **spring** function. The first is the component we will use to wrap the elements we want to animate, while the function is a utility that can interpolate a value from its initial state to the final one:

```
import { Motion, spring } from 'react-motion'
```

Let's look at the code:

```
const Transition = () => (
  <Motion
    defaultStyle={{ opacity: 0.01 }}
    style={{ opacity: spring(1) }}
  >
    {interpolatingStyle => (
      <h1 style={interpolatingStyle}>Hello React</h1>
    )}
  </Motion>
)
```

There are a lot of interesting things here.

First, you may have noticed that this component uses the function as a child pattern (see Chapter 4, *Compose all the Things*), which is a pretty powerful technique to define children that receive values at runtime.

Then we can see that the Motion component has two attributes: the first one is defaultStyle, which represents the initial style.

Again, we set the opacity to 0.0.1 to hide the element and start the fade.

The style attribute represents the final style instead, but we do not set the value directly; we use the spring function, so the value is interpolated from the initial state to the final one.

On each iteration of the spring function, the child function receives the interpolated style for the given point in time and, just by applying the received object to the style attribute of the component, we can see the transition of the opacity.

This library can do some more cool stuff, but the first things to learn are the basic concepts, and this example should clarify them.

It is also interesting to compare the two different approaches of the transition group and `react-motion` to be able to choose the right one for the project you are working on.

Scalable Vector Graphics

Last but not least, one of the most interesting techniques we can apply in the browser to draw icons and graphs is **Scalable Vector Graphics** (**SVG**).

SVG is great, because it is a declarative way of describing vectors and it fits perfectly with the purposes of React.

We used to use icon fonts to create icons, but they have well-known problems, with the first being that they are not accessible. It is also pretty hard to position icon fonts with CSS, and they do not always look beautiful in all browsers. These are the reasons we should prefer SVG for our web applications.

From a React point of view, it does not make any difference if we output a `div` or an SVG element from the render method, and this is what makes it so powerful.

We tend also to choose SVGs because we can easily modify them at runtime using CSS and JavaScript, which makes them an excellent candidate for the functional approach of React.

So, if we think about our components as a function of their props, we can easily imagine how we can create self-contained SVG icons that we can manipulate passing different props to them.

A common way to create SVGs in a web app with React is to wrap our vectors into a React component and use the props to define their dynamic values.

Let's look at a simple example where we draw a blue circle, creating a React component which wraps an SVG element:

```
const Circle = ({ x, y, radius, fill }) => (
  <svg>
    <circle cx={x} cy={y} r={radius} fill={fill} />
  </svg>
)
```

As you can see, we can easily use a stateless functional component which wraps the SVG markup, and it accepts the same props as the SVG does.

So, the SVG is just a template, and we can use the same `Circle` multiple times in our application, with various props.

The props are defined in the following way:

```
Circle.propTypes = {
  x: React.PropTypes.number,
  y: React.PropTypes.number,
  radius: React.PropTypes.number,
  fill: React.PropTypes.string,
}
```

This is great, because it makes working with SVGs and their properties more explicit so that the interface is clear and we know exactly how to configure our icons.

An example usage is as follows:

```
<Circle x={20} y={20} radius={20} fill="blue" />
```

We can obviously use the full power of React and set some default parameters so that, if the Circle icon is rendered without props, we still show something.

For example, we can define the default color:

```
Circle.defaultProps = {
  fill: 'red',
}
```

This is pretty powerful when we build UIs, especially in a team where we share our icon set and we want to have some default values in it, but we also want to let other teams decide their settings without having to recreate the same SVG shapes.

However, in some cases, we prefer to be more strict and fix some values to keep consistency. With React, that is a super simple task.

For example, we can wrap the base circle component into a `RedCircle`, as follows:

```
const RedCircle = ({ x, y, radius }) => (
  <Circle x={x} y={y} radius={radius} fill="red" />
)
```

Here, the color is set by default and it cannot be changed, while the other props are transparently passed to the original circle.

The prop types are the same without the fill:

```
RedCircle.propTypes = {
  x: React.PropTypes.number,
  y: React.PropTypes.number,
  radius: React.PropTypes.number,
}
```

The screenshot shows two circles, blue and red, generated by React using SVG:

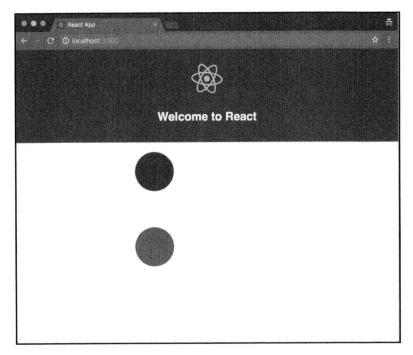

We can apply this technique and create different variations of the circle, such as SmallCircle and RightCircle, and everything else we need to build our UIs.

Summary

In this chapter, we have looked at different things we can do when we target the browser with React, from form creation to events, and from animations to SVGs.

React gives us a declarative way to manage all the aspects we need to deal with when we create a web application.

In case we need it, React gives us access to the actual DOM nodes in a way that we can perform imperative operations with them, which is useful if we need to integrate React with an existing imperative library.

The following chapter will be about CSS and inline styles, and it will clarify what it means to write CSS in JavaScript.

7
Make Your Components Look Beautiful

Our journey into React best practices and design patterns has now reached the point where we want to make our components look beautiful. To do that, we will go through all the reasons why regular CSS may not be the best approach for styling components, and we will check out various alternative solutions.

Starting with inline styles, then Radium, CSS Modules, and Styled Components, this chapter will guide you into the magical world of CSS in JavaScript.

The topic is very hot and highly controversial, so this chapter requires an open mind in order to be understood and followed.

In this chapter, we will cover the following:

- Common problems with regular CSS at scale
- What it means to use inline styles in React and the downsides
- How the Radium library can help fix issues of inline styles
- How to set up a project from scratch using Webpack and CSS Modules
- Features of CSS Modules and why they represent a great solution to avoid global CSS
- Styled Components, a new library that offers a modern approach to styling React components

CSS in JS

In the community, everyone agrees that a revolution took place in the styling of React components in November 2014, when *Christopher Chedeau* gave a talk at the NationJS conference.

Also known as *Vjeux* on the Internet, *Christopher* works at Facebook and contributes to React. In his talk, he went through all the problems related to CSS at scale that they were facing at Facebook.

It is worth understanding all of them, because some are pretty common and they will help us introduce concepts such as **inline styles** and **locally scoped class names**.

The following slide, taken from the presentation, lists the main issues with CSS:

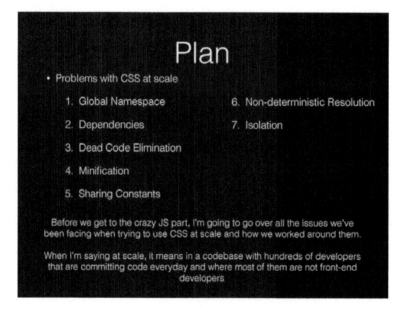

The first well-known problem of CSS is that all the selectors are global. No matter how we organize our styles, using namespaces or a BEM-like methodology, in the end, we are always polluting the global namespace, which we all know is wrong. It is not only wrong on principle, but it also leads to many errors in big codebases, and it makes maintainability very hard in the long term. Working with big teams, it is non-trivial to know if a particular class or element has already been styled, and most of the time we tend to add more classes instead of reusing existing ones.

The second problem with CSS regards the definition of the dependencies. It is very hard, in fact, to clearly state that a particular component depends on a specific CSS and that the CSS has to be loaded for the style to be applied. Since styles are global, any style from any file can be applied to any element, and losing control is very easy.

Frontend developers tend to use pre-processors to be able to split their CSS into sub-modules, but in the end a big, global CSS bundle is generated for the browser. Since CSS codebases tend to become huge quickly, we lose control over them, and the third problem is to do with **dead code elimination**. It is not easy to quickly identify which styles belong to which component, and this makes deleting code incredibly hard. In fact, due to the cascading nature of CSS, removing a selector or a rule can result in an unintended result within the browser.

Another pain of working with CSS concerns the minification of the selectors and the class names, both in the CSS and in the JavaScript application. It could seem an easy task, but it is not, especially when classes are applied on the fly or concatenated in the client.

Not being able to minify and optimize class names is pretty bad for performance, and it can make a huge difference to the size of the CSS.

Another pretty common operation that is non-trivial with regular CSS is sharing constants between the styles and the client application. We often need to know the height of a header, for example, to recalculate the position of other elements that depend on it.

Usually, we read the value in the client using the JavaScript APIs, but the optimal solution would be to share constants and avoid doing expensive calculations at runtime. This represents the fifth problem that Vjeux and the other developers at Facebook tried to solve.

The sixth issue concerns the non-deterministic resolution of CSS. In fact, in CSS, the order matters and if the CSS is loaded on-demand, the order is not guaranteed which leads to the wrong styles being applied to the elements.

Suppose, for example, that we want to optimize the way we request CSS, loading the CSS related to a particular page only when the users navigate to it. If the CSS related to this last page has some rules that also apply to the elements of different pages, the fact that it has been loaded last could affect the styling of the rest of the app. For example, if the user goes back to the previous page, they might see a page with a UI that is slightly different than the first time they visited it.

It is incredibly hard to control all the various combinations of styles, rules, and navigation paths, but again, being able to load the CSS when needed could have a critical impact on the performance of a web application.

Last but not least, the seventh problem of CSS, according to *Christopher Chedeau*, is related to isolation. In CSS, in fact, it is almost impossible to achieve a proper isolation between files or components. Selectors are global, and they can easily be overwritten. It is tricky to predict the final style of an element just by knowing the class names applied to it, because styles are not isolated and other rules in other parts of the application can affect unrelated elements.

I strongly recommend everyone check out this talk if you want to know more about the topic, because even if it sounds a bit strong and controversial, it is very inspiring and it forces you to approach the styling topic with an open mind:

```
https://vimeo.com/116209150
```

The conclusion of the talk is that to solve all the problems with CSS at scale at Facebook, they ended up using *inline styles.*

In the following section, we will look at what it means to use inline styles with React and the benefits and downsides of it.

Inline styles

The official React documentation suggests developers use inline styles to style their React components. This seems odd, because we all learned in past years that separating the concerns is important and we should not mix markup and CSS.

React tries to change the concept of separation of concerns by moving it from separation of technologies to separation of components. Separating markup, styling, and logic into different files when they are tightly coupled and where cannot work one without the other is just an illusion. Even if it helps keep the project structure cleaner, it does not give any real benefit.

In React, we compose components to create applications where components are a fundamental unit of our structure. We should be able to move components across the application, and they should provide the same result regarding both logic and UI, no matter where they get rendered.

This is one of the reasons why co-locating the styles within our components and applying them using inline styles on the elements could make sense in React.

First, let's look at an example of what it means to use the style attribute of the nodes to apply the styling to our components in React.

We are going to create a button with the text **Click me!**, and we are going to apply a color and a background color to it:

```
const style = {
  color: 'palevioletred',
  backgroundColor: 'papayawhip',
}

const Button = () => <button style={style}>Click me!</button>
```

As you can see, it is pretty easy to style elements with inline styles in React. We just have to create an object where the attributes are the CSS rules and the values are the values we would use in a regular CSS file.

The only differences are that the hyphenated CSS rules must be camelCased to be JavaScript-compliant, and the values are strings, so they have to be wrapped into quote marks.

There are some exceptions regarding the vendor prefixes. For example, if we want to define a transition on **webkit**, we should use the WebkitTransition attribute, where the webkit prefix begins with a capital letter. This rule applies to all the vendor prefixes, except for **ms**, which is lowercase.

Other use cases are numbers: they can be written without quotes or units of measurement and, by default, they are treated as pixels.

The following rule applies a height of 100px:

```
const style = {
  height: 100,
}
```

Using inline styles works, and we can also do things that are hard to implement with regular CSS. For example, we can recalculate some CSS values on the client at runtime, which is a very powerful concept, as you will see in the following example.

Suppose you want to create a form field in which the font size changes according to its value. So, if the value of the field is 24, the font size is going to be 24 pixels. With normal CSS, this behavior is almost impossible to reproduce without putting in huge effort and duplicated code.

Let's look at how easy it is to use inline styles instead.

We create a class because we have to store the state, and we need an event handler:

```
class FontSize extends React.Component
```

The class has a constructor, where we set the default value for the state, and we bind the `handleChange` handler, which listens to the `onChange` event of the input field:

```
constructor(props) {
  super(props)

  this.state = {
    value: 16,
  }

  this.handleChange = this.handleChange.bind(this)
}
```

We implement a simple change handler, where we use the target attribute of the event to retrieve the current value of the field:

```
handleChange({ target }) {
  this.setState({
    value: Number(target.value),
  })
}
```

Finally, we render the input file of type number, which is a controlled component because we keep its value updated by using the state. It also has an event handler, which is fired every time the value of the field changes.

Last but not least, we use the style attribute of the field to set its `font-size`. As you can see, we are using the camelCased version of the CSS rule to follow the React convention:

```
render() {
  return (
    <input
      type="number"
      value={this.state.value}
      onChange={this.handleChange}
      style={{ fontSize: this.state.value }}
    />
  )
}
```

Rendering the preceding component, we can see an input field, which changes its font size according to its value. The way it works is that when the value changes, we store the new value of the field inside the state. Modifying the state forces the component to re-render, and we use the new state value to set the display value of the field and its font size: easy and powerful.

Every solution in computer science has its downsides, and it always represents a trade-off. In the case of inline styles, unfortunately, the problems are many.

For example, with inline styles, it is not possible to use pseudo selectors (for example, `:hover`) and pseudo elements, which is a pretty significant limitation if you are creating a UI with interactions and animations.

There are some workarounds, and for example, you can always create real elements instead of pseudo ones, but for the pseudo classes, it is necessary to use JavaScript to simulate the CSS behavior, which is not optimal.

The same applies to **Media queries**, which cannot be defined using inline styles and it makes it harder to create responsive web applications. Since styles are declared using JavaScript objects, it is also not possible to use style fallbacks:

```
display: -webkit-flex;
display: flex;
```

JavaScript objects, in fact, cannot have two attributes with the same name. Style fallbacks should be avoided, but it is always good to have the ability to use them if needed.

Another feature of CSS it is not possible to emulate using inline styles is **Animations**. The workaround here is to define animations globally and use them inside the style attribute of the elements.

With inline styles, whenever we need to override a style with regular CSS, we are always forced to use the `!important` keyword, which is a bad practice because it prevents any other style being applied to the element.

The most difficult thing that happens working with inline styles is debugging. In fact, we tend to use class names to find elements in the browser DevTools to debug and check which styles have been applied.

With inline styles, all the styles of the items are listed in their style attribute, which makes it very hard to check and debug the result.

For example, the button that we created earlier in this section is rendered in the following way:

```
<button style="color: palevioletred; background-color: papayawhip; ">Click
me!</button>
```

By itself, it does not seem very hard to read, but if you imagine you have hundreds of elements and hundreds of styles, you realize that the problem becomes very complicated.

Also, if you are debugging a list where every single item has the same style attribute, and if you modify one on the fly to check the result in the browser, you will see that you are applying the styles only to it and not to all the other siblings, even if they share the same style.

Last but not least, if we render our application on the server side (we will cover this topic in Chapter 8, *Server-Side Rendering for Fun and Profit*), the size of the page is bigger when using inline styles.

With inline styles, we are putting all the content of the CSS into the markup, which adds an extra number of bytes to the file that we send to the clients and makes the web application appear slower.

Compression algorithms can help with that because they can easily compress similar patterns, and, in some cases, loading the critical path CSS is a good solution, but in general we should try to avoid it.

It turns out that inline styles give more problems than the problems they try to solve.

For this reason, the community created different tools to solve the problems of inline styles but keeping the styles inside the components, or local to the components, to get the best of both worlds.

After *Christopher Chedeau's* talk, a lot of developers started talking about inline styles, and many solutions and experiments have been made to find new ways of writing CSS in JavaScript.

I personally decided to try all of them, and I created a repository where I publish a small button component built with each one of the available solutions:

```
https://github.com/MicheleBertoli/css-in-js
```

In the beginning, there were two or three, while today there are more than forty.

In the following sections, we will go through the most popular ones.

Radium

One of the first libraries created to solve the problems of inline styles we have encountered in the previous section is **Radium**. It is maintained by the great developers at *Formidable Labs*, and it is still one of the most popular solutions.

In this section, we will look at how Radium works, which problems it solves, and why it is a great library to use in conjunction with React for styling components.

We are going to create a very simple button, similar to the one we built in the example earlier in this chapter.

We will start with a basic button without styling, and we will add some basic styling, as well as pseudo classes and Media queries, to it in order to learn the main features of the library.

The button we will start with is as follows:

```
const Button = () => <button>Click me!</button>
```

First, we have to install Radium using npm:

```
npm install --save radium
```

Once the installation is complete, we can import the library and wrap the button into it:

```
import radium from 'radium'

const Button = () => <button>Click me!</button>

export default radium(Button)
```

The radium function is a **Higher-Order Component** (see Chapter 4, *Compose all the Things*), which extends the functionalities of our Button, returning a new enhanced component.

If we render the button inside the browser, we will not see anything in particular at the moment, because we are not applying any styles to it.

Let's start with a very simple style object, where we set the background color, the padding, the size, and a couple of other CSS properties.

As we have seen in the previous section, inline styles in React are defined using JavaScript objects with camelCased CSS properties:

```
const styles = {
  backgroundColor: '#ff0000',
  width: 320,
  padding: 20,
  borderRadius: 5,
  border: 'none',
  outline: 'none',
}
```

The preceding snippet is no different from plain inline styles with React, and if we pass it to our button as follows, we can see all the styles applied to the button inside the browser:

```
const Button = () => <button style={styles}>Click me!</button>
```

The result is the following markup:

```
<button data-radium="true" style="background-color: rgb(255, 0, 0); width:
320px; padding: 20px; border-radius: 5px; border: none; outline:
none;">Click me!</button>
```

The only difference you can see here is that there is a data-radium attribute set to `true` attached to the element.

Now, we have seen that inline styles do not let us define any pseudo classes; let's take a look at how to solve the problem using Radium.

Using pseudo-classes, such as `:hover`, with Radium is pretty straightforward.

We have to create a `:hover` property inside our style object, and Radium will do the rest:

```
const styles = {
  backgroundColor: '#ff0000',
  width: 320,
  padding: 20,
  borderRadius: 5,
  border: 'none',
  outline: 'none',
  ':hover': {
    color: '#fff',
  },
}
```

If you apply this style object to your button and render it on the screen, you can see that passing the mouse over the button results in a button with white text, as opposed to the default black one.

That is great: we can use pseudo classes and inline styles together.

However, if you open your DevTools and try to force the `:hover` status in the **Styles** panel, you will see that nothing happens.

The reason you can see the hover effect but you cannot simulate it with CSS, is that Radium uses JavaScript to apply and remove the hover state defined in the style object.

If you hover over the element with the DevTools open, you can see that the style string changes and the color gets added to it dynamically:

```
<button data-radium="true" style="background-color: rgb(255, 0, 0); width:
320px; padding: 20px; border-radius: 5px; border: none; outline: none;
color: rgb(255, 255, 255);">Click me!</button>
```

The way Radium works is by adding an event handler for each one of the events that can trigger the behavior of pseudo classes, and listening to them.

As soon as one of the events gets fired, Radium changes the state of the component, which re-renders with the right style for the state. This might seem weird in the beginning, but there are no real downsides to this approach, and the difference in terms of performance is not perceivable.

We can add new pseudo-classes, for example, `:active`, and they will work as well:

```
const styles = {
  backgroundColor: '#ff0000',
  width: 320,
  padding: 20,
  borderRadius: 5,
  border: 'none',
  outline: 'none',
  ':hover': {
    color: '#fff',
  },
  ':active': {
    position: 'relative',
    top: 2,
  },
}
```

Another critical feature that Radium enables is Media queries. Media queries are crucial for creating responsive applications, and Radium again uses JavaScript to enable that CSS feature in our application.

Let's look at how it works: the API is pretty similar; we just have to create a new attribute on our style object and nest the styles that must be applied when the media query matches inside it:

```
const styles = {
  backgroundColor: '#ff0000',
  width: 320,
  padding: 20,
  borderRadius: 5,
  border: 'none',
  outline: 'none',
  ':hover': {
    color: '#fff',
  },
  ':active': {
    position: 'relative',
    top: 2,
  },
  '@media (max-width: 480px)': {
    width: 160,
  },
}
```

There is one thing we must do to make Media queries work, and that is wrapping our application into the StyleRoot component provided by Radium.

For the Media queries to work properly, especially with server-side rendering, Radium will inject the rules related to the media query in a style element inside the DOM, with all the properties set as !important.

This is to avoid flickering between the different styles applied to the document before the library figures out which is the matching query. Implementing the styles inside a style element prevents this by letting the browser do its regular job.

So, the idea is to import the StyleRoot component:

```
import { StyleRoot } from 'radium'
```

And wrap our entire application inside it:

```
class App extends Component {
  render() {
    return (
      <StyleRoot>
        ...
      </StyleRoot>
    )
  }
}
```

As a result of this, if you open the DevTools, you can see that Radium injected the following style into the DOM:

```
<style>@media (max-width: 480px){ .rmq-1d8d7428{width: 160px
!important;}}</style>
```

The `rmq-1d8d7428` class has been applied to the button automatically, as well:

```
<button class="rmq-1d8d7428" data-radium="true" style="background-color:
rgb(255, 0, 0); width: 320px; padding: 20px; border-radius: 5px; border:
none; outline: none;">Click me!</button>
```

If you now resize the browser window, you can see that the button becomes smaller for small screens, as expected.

CSS Modules

If you feel that inline styles are not a suitable solution for your project and your team, but you still want to keep the styles as close as possible to your components, there is a solution for you, called **CSS Modules**.

Webpack

Before diving into CSS Modules and learning how it works, it is important to understand how it was created and the tools that support it.

In `Chapter 2`, *Clean Up Your Code*, we looked at how we can write ES2015 code and transpile it using Babel and its presets. As soon as the application grows, you may want to split your code base into modules as well.

To divide the application into small modules that you can import whenever you need them, while still creating a big bundle for the browser, you can use a tool such as **Browserify** or **Webpack**. These tools are called **module bundlers**, and what they do is load all the dependencies of your application into a single bundle that can be executed in the browser, which does not have any concept of modules (yet).

Webpack is especially popular in the React world because it offers many interesting and useful features, with the first one being the concept of loaders. With Webpack, in fact, you can potentially load any dependencies other than JavaScript, if there is a loader for it. For example, you can load JSON files, as well as images and other assets, inside the bundle.

In May 2015, *Mark Dalgleish*, one of the creators of CSS Modules, figured out that you could import CSS inside a Webpack bundle as well, and he pushed the concept forward.

He thought that, since the CSS could be imported locally to a component, all the imported class names could be locally scoped as well. The concept is clearly explained in an article entitled *The end of global CSS*:

https://medium.com/seek-ui-engineering/the-end-of-global-css-90d2a4a06284

Setting up a project

In this section, we will look at how to set up a very simple Webpack application, using Babel to transpile the JavaScript and the CSS Modules to load our locally scoped CSS into the bundle. We will also go through all the features of CSS Modules and look at the problems they can solve. The first thing to do is move to an empty folder and run the following:

```
npm init
```

This will create a `package.json` with some defaults.

Now it is time to install the dependencies, with the first one being Webpack and the second, `webpack-dev-server`, which we will use to run the application locally and to create the bundle on the fly:

```
npm install --save-dev webpack webpack-dev-server
```

Once Webpack is installed, it is time to install Babel and its loader. Since we are using Webpack to create the bundle, we will use the Babel loader to transpile our ES2015 code within Webpack itself:

```
npm install  --save-dev babel-loader babel-core babel-preset-es2015
babel-preset-react
```

Finally, we install the style loader and the CSS loader, which are the two loaders we need to enable the CSS Modules:

```
npm install --save-dev style-loader CSS-loader
```

There is one more thing to do to make things easier, and that is install the `html-webpack-plugin`, which is a plugin that can create an HTML page to host our JavaScript application on the fly, just by looking into the Webpack configuration and without us needing to create a regular file:

```
npm install --save-dev html-webpack-plugin
```

Last but not least, we install `react` and `react-dom` to use them in our simple example:

```
npm install --save react react-dom
```

Now that all the dependencies are installed, it is time to configure everything to make it work.

The first thing to do is to add an `npm` script in the `package.json` to run the `webpack-dev-server`, which will serve the application in development:

```
"scripts": {
  "start": "webpack-dev-server"
},
```

Webpack needs a configuration file to know how to handle the different types of dependencies we are using in our application, and to do so we create a file called `webpack.config.js`, which exports an object:

```
module.exports = { }
```

The object we export represents the configuration object used by Webpack to create the bundle, and it can have different properties depending on the size and the features of the project.

We want to keep our example very simple, so we are going to add three attributes.

The first one is entry, which tells Webpack where the main file of our application is:

```
entry: './index.js',
```

The second one is module, which is where we tell Webpack how to load the external dependencies. It has an attribute called `loaders`, where we set a specific loader for each one of the file types:

```
module: {
  loaders: [
    {
      test: /\.js$/,
      exclude: /(node_modules|bower_components)/,
      loader: 'babel',
      query: {
        presets: ['es2015', 'react'],
      }
    },
    {
      test: /\.css$/,
      loader: 'style!css?modules',
    },
  ],
},
```

We are saying that the files that match the `.js` regex are loaded using the `babel-loader` so that they get transpiled and loaded into the bundle.

You may also have noticed that we are setting the presets in there as well. As we have seen in Chapter 2, *Clean Up Your Code*, the presets are sets of configuration options that instruct Babel on how to deal with the different types of syntax (for example, JSX).

The second entry in the `loaders` array tells Webpack what to do when a CSS file is imported, and it uses the css-loader with the `modules` flag enabled to activate CSS Modules. The result of the transformation is then passed to the style loader, which injects the styles into the head of the page.

Finally, we enable the HTML plugin in order to generate the page for us, adding the script tag automatically using the entry path we specified earlier:

```
const HtmlWebpackPlugin = require('html-webpack-plugin')
...
plugins: [new HtmlWebpackPlugin()]
```

We are done, and if we run `npm` start in the terminal and point the browser to `http://localhost:8080`, we should be able to see the following markup being served:

```
<!DOCTYPE html>
<html>
  <head>
    <meta charset="UTF-8">
    <title>Webpack App</title>
  </head>
  <body>
    <script type="text/javascript" src="bundle.js"></script></body>
</html>
```

Locally scoped CSS

Now it is time to create our app, which will consist of a simple button, the same we used in the previous examples. We will use it to show all the features of the CSS Modules.

Let's create an `index.js` file, which is the entry we specified in the Webpack configuration, and let's import `React` and `ReactDOM` as well:

```
import React from 'react'
import ReactDOM from 'react-dom'
```

We then create the simple button. As usual, we are going to start with a non-styled button, and we will add the styles step-by-step:

```
const Button = () => <button>Click me!</button>
```

Finally, we render the button into the DOM:

```
ReactDOM.render(<Button />, document.body)
```

Please note that rendering a React component into the body is a bad practice, but in this case, we are doing it for simplicity.

Now, suppose we want to apply some styles to the button: a background color, the size, and so on.

We create a regular CSS file, called `index.css`, and we put the following class into it:

```
.button {
  background-color: #ff0000;
  width: 320px;
  padding: 20px;
  border-radius: 5px;
```

```
  border: none;
  outline: none;
}
```

Now, we said that with CSS Modules we could import the CSS files into the JavaScript; let's look at how it works.

Inside our `index.js` where we defined the button component, we can add the following line:

```
import styles from './index.css'
```

The result of this `import` statement is a styles object, where all the attributes are the classes defined in the `index.css`.

If we run `console.log` (styles), we can see the following object in DevTools:

```
{
  button: "_2wpxM3yizfwbWee6k0UlD4"
}
```

So, we have an object where the attributes are the class names and the values are (apparently) random strings. We will see later that they are non-random, but let's check first what we can do with that object.

We can use the object to set the class name attribute of our button, as follows:

```
const Button = () => (
  <button className={styles.button}>Click me!</button>
)
```

If we go back to the browser, we can now see that the styles we defined in the `index.css` have been applied to the button.

And that is not magic, because if we check in DevTools, the class that has been applied to the element is the same string attached to the style object we imported inside our code:

```
<button class="_2wpxM3yizfwbWee6k0UlD4">Click me!</button>
```

If we look at the head section of the page, we can now see that the same class name has also been injected into the page:

```
<style type="text/css">
._2wpxM3yizfwbWee6k0UlD4 {
  background-color: #ff0000;
  width: 320px;
  padding: 20px;
```

```
      border-radius: 5px;
      border: none;
      outline: none;
    }
    </style>
```

This is how the CSS and the style loaders work.

The CSS loader lets you import the CSS files into your JavaScript modules and, when the modules flag is activated, all the class names are locally scoped to the module they are imported into.

As mentioned previously, the string we imported was non-random, but it is generated using the hash of the file and some other parameters in a way that is unique within the code base.

Finally, the style loader takes the result of the CSS Modules transformation and it injects the styles inside the head section of the page.

This is very powerful because we have the full power and expressivity of the CSS combined with the advantages of having locally scoped class names and explicit dependencies.

As mentioned at the beginning of the chapter, CSS is global, and that makes it very hard to maintain in large applications. With CSS Modules, class names are locally scoped and they cannot clash with other class names in different parts of the application, enforcing a deterministic result.

Moreover, explicitly importing the CSS dependencies inside our components helps us see clearly which components need which CSS. It is also very useful for eliminating dead code, because when we delete a component for any reason, we can tell exactly which CSS it was using.

CSS Modules are regular CSS, so we can use pseudo classes, Media queries, and animations.

For example, we can add CSS rules like the following:

```
    .button:hover {
      color: #fff;
    }

    .button:active {
      position: relative;
      top: 2px;
    }

    @media (max-width: 480px) {
```

```
  .button {
    width: 160px
  }
}
```

This will be transformed into the following code and injected into the document:

```
._2wpxM3yizfwbWee6k0UlD4:hover {
  color: #fff;
}

._2wpxM3yizfwbWee6k0UlD4:active {
  position: relative;
  top: 2px;
}

@media (max-width: 480px) {
  ._2wpxM3yizfwbWee6k0UlD4 {
    width: 160px
  }
}
```

The class names get created and they get replaced everywhere the button is used, making it reliable and local, as expected.

As you may have noticed, those class names are great, but they make debugging pretty hard, because we cannot easily tell which classes generated the hash.

What we can do in development mode is add a special configuration parameter, with which we can choose the pattern used to produce the scoped class names.

For example, we can change the value of the loader as follows:

```
loader: 'style!css?modules&localIdentName=[local]--[hash:base64:5]',
```

Here, `localIdentName` is the parameter and `[local]` and `[hash:base64:5]` are placeholders for the original class name value and a five-character hash.

Other available placeholders are [path], which represents the path of the CSS file, and [name], which is the name of the source CSS file.

Activating the previous configuration option, the result we have in the browser is as follows:

```
<button class="button--2wpxM">Click me!</button>
```

This is way more readable and easier to debug.

In production, we do not need class names like this, and we are more interested in performance, so we may want shorter class names and hashes.

With Webpack, it is pretty straightforward because we can have multiple configuration files that can be used in the different stages of our application life cycle. Also, in production, we may want to extract the CSS file instead of injecting it into the browser from the bundle so that we can have a lighter bundle and cache the CSS on a CDN for better performance.

To do that, you need to install another Webpack plugin, called `extract-text-plugin`, which can write an actual CSS file, putting all the scoped classes generated from CSS Modules.

There are a couple of features of CSS Modules that are worth mentioning.

The first one is the **global** keyword. Prefixing any class with `:global`, in fact, means asking CSS Modules not to scope the current selector locally.

For example, change our CSS as follows:

```
:global .button {
  . . .
}
```

The output will be the following:

```
.button {
  . . .
}
```

That is good if you want to apply styles which cannot be scoped locally, such as third-party widgets.

My favorite feature of CSS Modules is **composition**. With composition, we can reference classes from the same file or external dependencies and get all the styles applied to the element.

For example, extract the rule to set the background to red from the rules of the button into a separate block, as follows:

```
.background-red {
  background-color: #ff0000;
}
```

We can then compose it inside our button in the following way:

```
.button {
  composes: background-red;
  width: 320px;
  padding: 20px;
  border-radius: 5px;
  border: none;
  outline: none;
}
```

The result is that all the rules of the button and all the rules of the `composes` declaration are applied to the element.

This is a very powerful feature and it works in a fascinating way. You might expect that all the composed classed are duplicated inside the classes where they are referenced as SASS `@extend` does, but that is not the case. Simply, all the composed class names are applied one after the other on the component in the DOM.

In our specific case, we would have the following:

```
<button class="_2wpxM3yizfwbWee6k0U1D4 Sf8w9cFdQXdRV_i9dgcOq">Click
me!</button>
```

Here, the CSS that is injected into the page is as follows:

```
.Sf8w9cFdQXdRV_i9dgcOq {
  background-color: #ff0000;
}

._2wpxM3yizfwbWee6k0U1D4 {
  width: 320px;
  padding: 20px;
  border-radius: 5px;
  border: none;
  outline: none;
}
```

Atomic CSS Modules

It should be clear how composition works and why it is a very powerful feature of CSS Modules. At YPlan, the company where I worked when I started writing this book, we tried to push it a step forward, combining the power of `composes` with the flexibility of **Atomic CSS** (also known as **Functional CSS**).

Atomic CSS is a way to use CSS where every class has a single rule.

For example, we can create a class to set the margin bottom to zero:

```
.mb0 {
  margin-bottom: 0;
}
```

We can use another one to set the font-weight to six hundred:

```
.fw6 {
  font-weight: 600;
}
```

Then, we apply all those atomic classes to the elements:

```
<h2 class="mb0 fw6">Hello React</h2>
```

This technique is controversial, and particularly efficient at the same time. It is hard to start using it because you end up having too many classes in your markup, which makes it hard to predict the final result. If you think about it, it is pretty similar to inline styles, because you apply one class per rule, apart from the fact that you are using a shorter class name as a proxy.

The biggest argument against Atomic CSS is usually that you are moving the styling logic from the CSS to the markup, which is wrong. Classes are defined in CSS files, but they are composed in the views, and every time you have to modify the style of an element, you end up editing the markup.

On the other hand, we tried using Atomic CSS for a bit and we found out that it makes prototyping incredibly fast.

In fact, when all the base rules have been generated, applying those classes to the elements and creating new styles is a very quick process, which is good. Second, using Atomic CSS, we can control the size of the CSS file, because as soon as we create new components with their styles, we are using existing classes and we do not need to create new ones, which is great for performance.

So, we tried to solve the problems of Atomic CSS using CSS Modules and we called the technique **Atomic CSS Modules**.

In essence, you start creating your base CSS classes (for example, mb0) and then, instead of applying the class names one by one in the markup, you compose them into placeholder classes using CSS Modules.

Let's look at an example:

```
.title {
  composes: mb0 fw6;
}
```

Then:

```
<h2 className={styles.title}>Hello React</h2>
```

This is great, because you still keep the styling logic inside the CSS, and CSS Modules `composes` does the job for you by applying all the single classes into the markup.

The result of the preceding code is something like the following:

```
<h2 class="title--3JCJR mb0--21SyP fw6--1JRhZ">Hello React</h2>
```

Here, `title`, `mb0`, and `fw6` are all applied automatically to the element. They are scoped locally as well, so we have all the advantages of CSS Modules.

React CSS Modules

Last but not least, there is a great library that can help us work with CSS Modules. You may have noticed how we were using a style object to load all the classes of the CSS, and because JavaScript does not support hyphenated attributes, we are forced to use a camel-cased class name.

Also, if we are referencing a class name that does not exist in the CSS file, there is no way to know it, and `undefined` is added to the list of classes.

For these and other useful features, we may want to try a package which makes working with CSS Modules even smoother.

Let's look at what it means to go back to the `index.js` we were using previously in this section with plain CSS Modules, and change it to use React CSS Modules instead.

The package is called `react-css-modules`, and the first thing we must do is install it:

```
npm install --save react-css-modules
```

Once the package is installed, we import it inside our `index.js`:

```
import cssModules from 'react-css-modules'
```

We use it as a Higher-Order Component, passing to it the `Button` component we want to enhance and the styles object we imported from the CSS:

```
const EnhancedButton = cssModules(Button, styles)
```

Now we have to change the implementation of the button to avoid using the styles object. With React CSS Modules we use the `styleName` property, which is transformed into a regular class.

The great thing is that we can use the class name as a string (for example, `"button"`):

```
const Button = () => <button styleName="button">Click me!</button>
```

If we now render the `EnhancedButton` into the DOM, we will see that nothing has really changed from before, which means that the library works.

If we try to change the `styleName` property to reference a non-existing class name, as follows:

```
const Button = () => (
  <button styleName="button1">Click me!</button>
)
```

We will see the following error in the console of the browser:

```
Uncaught Error: "button1" CSS module is undefined.
```

This is particularly helpful when the codebase grows and we have multiple developers working on different components and styles.

Styled Components

There is a library which is very promising, because it takes into account all the problems the other libraries have encountered in styling components.

Different paths have been followed for writing CSS in JavaScript, and many solutions have been tried, so now the time is ripe for a library that takes all the learning and then builds something on top of it.

The library is conceived and maintained by two popular developers in the JavaScript community: *Glenn Maddern* and *Max Stoiberg*.

It represents a very modern approach to the problem, and it uses edge features of ES2015 and some advanced techniques applied to React to provide a complete solution for styling.

Let's look at how it is possible to create the same button we saw in the previous sections, and check if all the CSS features we are interested in (for example, pseudo classes and Media queries) work with Styled Components.

First, we have to install the library by running the following command:

```
npm install --save styled-components
```

Once the library is installed, we have to import it inside our component's file:

```
import styled from 'styled-components'
```

At that point, we can use the styled function to create any element by doing `styled.elementName`, where `elementName` can be a `div`, a button, or any other valid DOM element.

The second thing to do is define the style of the element we are creating, and to do so, we use a ES2015 feature called **Tagged Template Literals**, which is a way of passing template strings to a function without them being interpolated beforehand.

This means that the function receives the actual template with all the JavaScript expressions, and this makes the library able to use the full power of JavaScript to apply the styles to the elements.

Let's start by creating a simple button with a basic styling:

```
const Button = styled.button
  backgroundColor: #ff0000;
  width: 320px;
  padding: 20px;
  borderRadius: 5px;
```

[180]

```
    border: none;
    outline: none;
`
```

This kind-of-weird syntax returns a proper React component called `Button`, which renders a button element and applies to it all the styles defined in the template. The way the styles are applied is first by creating a unique class name, adding it to the element, and then injecting the corresponding style in the head of the document.

The following is the component that gets rendered:

```
<button class="kYvFOg">Click me!</button>
```

The style that gets added to the page is as follows:

```
.kYvFOg {
    background-color: #ff0000;
    width: 320px;
    padding: 20px;
    border-radius: 5px;
    border: none;
    outline: none;
}
```

The good thing about Styled Components is that it supports almost all the features of CSS, which makes it a good candidate to be used in a real-world application.

For example, it supports pseudo classes using an SASS-like syntax:

```
const Button = styled.button`
  background-color: #ff0000;
  width: 320px;
  padding: 20px;
  border-radius: 5px;
  border: none;
  outline: none;
  &:hover {
    color: #fff;
  }
  &:active {
    position: relative;
    top: 2px;
  }
}
```

It also supports Media queries:

```
const Button = styled.button`
  background-color: #ff0000;
  width: 320px;
  padding: 20px;
  border-radius: 5px;
  border: none;
  outline: none;
  &:hover {
    color: #fff;
  }
  &:active {
    position: relative;
    top: 2px;
  }
  @media (max-width: 480px) {
    width: 160px;
  }
`
```

There are many other features that this library brings to your project.

For example, once you have created the button, you can easily override its styles and use it multiple times with different properties.

Inside the templates, it is also possible to use the props that the component received and change the style accordingly.

Another great feature is **Theming**. Wrapping your components into a ThemeProvider component, you can inject a theme property down to the three, which makes it extremely easy to create UIs where part of the style is shared between components and some other properties depend on the currently selected theme.

Summary

In this chapter, we have looked at a lot of interesting topics. We started by going through the problems of CSS at scale, specifically, the problems that they had at Facebook while dealing with CSS.

We learned how inline styles work in React and why it is good to co-locate the styles within components. We also looked at the limitations of inline styles.

Then, we moved to Radium, which solves the main problems of inline styles, giving us a clear interface to write our CSS in JavaScript. For those who think that inline styles are a bad solution, we moved into the world of CSS Modules, setting up a simple project from scratch.

Importing the CSS files into our components makes the dependencies clear, and scoping the class names locally avoids clashes. We have looked at how CSS Module's `composes` is a great feature, and how we can use it in conjunction with Atomic CSS to create a framework for quick prototyping.

Finally, we had a quick look at Styled Components, which is a very promising library and is meant to completely change the way we approach the styling of components.

8
Server-Side Rendering for Fun and Profit

The next step to building React applications is about learning how the server-side rendering works and which benefits it can give us. **Universal applications** are better for SEO, and they enable knowledge sharing between the frontend and the backend.

They can also improve the perceived speed of a web application, which usually leads to increased conversions. However, applying server-side rendering to a React application comes with a cost and we should think carefully about whether we really need it or not.

In this chapter, you will see how to set up a server-side rendered application, and by the end of the relevant sections, you will be able to build a Universal application and understand the pros and the cons of this technique.

In this chapter, we will cover the following:

- Understanding what a Universal application is
- Figuring out the reasons why we may want to enable server-side rendering
- Creating a simple static server-side rendered application with React
- Adding data fetching to server-side rendering and understanding concepts such as dehydration/hydration
- Using **Next.js** by Zeith to easily create a React application that runs on both the server and the client

Universal applications

When we talk about JavaScript web applications, we usually think of client-side code that lives in the browser.

The way they usually work is that the server returns an empty HTML page with a script tag to load the application. When the application is ready, it manipulates the DOM inside the browser to show the UI and to interact with users. This has been the case for the last few years, and it is still the way to go for a huge number of applications.

In this book, we have seen how easy it is to create applications using React components and how they work within the browser. What we have not seen yet is how React can render the same components on the server, giving us a powerful feature called **Server-Side Rendering (SSR)**.

Before going into the details, let's try to understand what it means to create applications that render both on the server and on the client. For years we used to have completely different applications for the server and client: for example, a Django application to render the views on the server, and some JavaScript frameworks, such as Backbone or jQuery, on the client. Those separate apps usually had to be maintained by two teams of developers with different skill sets. If you needed to share data between the server-side rendered pages and the client-side application, you could inject some variables inside a script tag. Using two different languages and platforms, there was no way to share common information such as models or views between the different sides of the application.

Since Node.js was released in 2009, JavaScript has gained a lot of attention and popularity on the server-side as well, thanks to web-application frameworks such as **Express**.

Using the same language on both sides not only makes it easy for developers to reuse their knowledge, it also enables different ways of sharing code between the server and the client.

With React in particular, the concept of isomorphic web applications became very popular within the JavaScript community.

Writing an **isomorphic application** means building an application that looks the same on the server and the client.

The fact that the same language is used to write the two applications means that a big part of the logic can be shared, which opens many possibilities. This makes the code base easier to reason about, and avoids unnecessary duplications.

React brings the concept a step forward, giving us a simple API to render our components on the server and transparently applying all the logic needed to make the page interactive (for example, event handlers) on the browser.

The term isomorphic does not fit in this scenario, because in the case of React the applications are exactly the same, and that is why one of the creators of React Router, *Michael Jackson*, proposed a more meaningful name for this pattern: *Universal*.

A Universal application is an application that can run both on the server and on the client-side with the same code.

In this chapter, we will look at the reasons why we should consider making our applications Universal, and we will learn how React components can be easily rendered on the server-side.

Reasons to implement Server-Side Rendering

SSR is a great feature, but we should not jump into it just for the sake of it: we should have a real and solid reason to start using it. In this section, we will look at how server-side rendering can help our application and which problems it can solve for us.

SEO

One of the main reasons we may want to render our applications on the server-side is **Search Engine Optimization (SEO)**.

In fact, if we serve an empty HTML skeleton to the crawlers of the main search engines, they are not able to extract any meaningful information from it.

Nowadays, Google seems to be able to run JavaScript, but there are some limitations, and SEO is often a critical aspect of our businesses.

For years, we used to write two applications: a server-side rendered one for the crawlers and another one to be used on the client side by the users.

We used to do that because server-side rendered applications could not give us the level of interactivity users expect, while a client-side application did not get indexed by search engines.

Maintaining and supporting two applications is difficult, and makes the code base less flexible and less prone to changes.

Luckily, with React, we can render our components on the server-side and serve the content of our applications to the crawlers in such a way that it is easy for them to understand and index the content.

This is great, not only for SEO, but also for social sharing services. In fact, platforms such as Facebook or Twitter give us a way of defining the content of the snippets that are shown when our pages are shared.

For example, using Open Graph, we can tell Facebook that, for a particular page, we want a certain image to be shown and a particular title to be used as the title of the post.

It is almost impossible to do that using client-side-only applications, because the engine that extracts the information from the pages uses the markup returned by the server.

If our server returns an empty HTML structure for all the URLs, the result is that, when the pages are shared on the social networks, the snippets of our web application are empty as well, which affects their virality.

A common code base

We do not have many options on the client: our applications have to be written in JavaScript. There are some languages that can be converted into JavaScript at build time, but the concept does not change.

The ability to use the same language on the server represents a significant win regarding maintainability and knowledge sharing across the company.

Being able to share the logic between the client and the server makes it easy to apply any changes on both sides without doing the work twice, which most of the time leads to fewer errors and fewer problems.

The effort of maintaining a single code base is less than the work required to keep two different applications up-to-date.

Another reason you might consider introducing JavaScript on the server-side in your team is sharing knowledge between frontend and backend developers.

The ability to reuse the code on both sides makes collaboration easier, and the teams speak a common language, which helps with making faster decisions and changes.

Better performance

Last but not least, we all love client-side applications, because they are fast and responsive, but there is a problem: the bundle has to be loaded and run before users can take any action on the application.

This might not be a problem using a modern laptop or a desktop computer on a fast Internet connection. However, if we load a huge JavaScript bundle using a mobile device with a 3G connection, users have to wait for a little while before interacting with the application. This is not only bad for the UX in general, but it also affects conversions. It has been proven by the major e-commerce websites that a few milliseconds added to the page load can have an enormous impact on revenues.

For example, if we serve our application with an empty HTML page and a `script` tag on the server, and we show a spinner to our users until they can click on anything, the perception of the speed of the website is highly affected.

If we render our website on the server-side instead, and the users start seeing some of the content as soon as they hit the page, they are more likely to stay, even if they have to wait the same amount of time before doing anything for real because the client-side bundle has to be loaded regardless of the SSR.

This perceived performance is something we can greatly improve using server-side rendering, because we can output our components on the server and return some information to the users straight-away.

Don't underestimate the complexity

Obviously, even if React provides an easy API to render components on the server, creating a Universal application has a cost. So, we should consider carefully before enabling it for one of the preceding reasons and check if our team is ready to support and maintain a Universal application.

In fact, as we will see in the coming sections, rendering components it is not the only task that needs to be done to create server-side rendered applications.

We have to set up and maintain a server with its routes and its logic, manage the server data flow, and so on. Potentially, we want to cache the content to serve the pages faster and carry out many other tasks that are required to maintain a fully functional Universal application.

For this reason, my suggestion is to build the client-side version first, and only when the web application is fully working on the server should you think about improving the experience by enabling SSR.

The SSR should be enabled on when strictly needed. For example, if you need SEO or if you need to customize the social sharing information, you should start thinking about it.

If you realize that your application takes a lot of time to fully load and you have already done all the optimization (see the following chapter for more about this topic), you can consider using server-side rendering to offer a better experience to your users and improve the perceived speed.

Christopher Pojer, a Facebook engineer, said on Twitter that they enabled the server-side rendering on Instagram only for SEO reasons because, in the case of a highly dynamic content website such as Instagram, SSR is not useful to improve the user's perception of the speed:

```
https://twitter.com/cpojer/status/711729444323332096
```

A basic example

We will now create a very simple server-side application to look at the steps that are needed to build a basic Universal setup.

It is going to be a minimal and simple set-up on purpose, because the goal here is to show how SSR works rather than providing a comprehensive solution or a boilerplate, even though you could use the example application as a starting point for a real-world application.

 This section assumes that all the concepts regarding JavaScript build tools, such as Webpack and its loaders, are clear, and it requires a little bit of knowledge of Node.js. As a JavaScript developer, it should be easy for you to follow this section, even if you have never seen a Node.js application before.

The application will consist of two parts:

- The server-side, where we will use **Express** to create a basic web server and serve an HTML page with the server-side rendered React application
- The client side, where we will render the application as usual, using `react-dom`.

Both sides of the application will be transpiled with Babel and bundled with Webpack before being run, which lets us use the full power of ES2015 and the modules both on Node.js and on the browser.

Let's start by moving into an empty folder and running the following to create a new package:

```
npm init
```

When the package.json has been created, it is time to install the dependencies. We can start with Webpack:

```
npm install --save-dev webpack
```

After it is done, it is time to install the Babel loader and the presets that we need in order to write an ES2015 application using React and JSX:

```
npm install --save-dev babel-loader babel-core babel-preset-es2015
babel-preset-react
```

We also have to install a dependency, which we will need to create the server bundle. Webpack lets us define a set of externals, which are dependencies that we do not want to add to the bundle. When creating a build for the server, in fact, we do not want to add to the bundle all the node packages that we use; we just want to bundle our server code. There's a package that helps with that, and we can simply apply it to the external entry in our Webpack configuration to exclude all the modules:

```
npm install --save-dev webpack-node-externals
```

Great, it is now time to create an entry in the npm scripts section of the `package.json` so that we can easily run the build command from the terminal:

```
"scripts": {
  "build": "webpack"
},
```

We now have to create the configuration file, called `webpack.config.js`, to tell Webpack how we want our files to be bundled.

Let's start importing the library we will use to set our node externals. We will also define the configuration for the Babel loader, which we will use for both the client and the server:

```
const nodeExternals = require('webpack-node-externals')

const loaders = [{
  test: /\.js$/,
  exclude: /(node_modules|bower_components)/,
```

```
    loader: 'babel',
    query: {
      presets: ['es2015', 'react'],
    },
  }]
```

In Chapter 7, *Make Your Components Look Beautiful,* we looked at how we had to export a configuration object from the configuration file. There is one cool feature in Webpack that lets us export an array of configurations as well so that we can define both client and server configurations in the same place and use both in one go.

The client configuration should be very familiar:

```
const client = {
  entry: './src/client.js',

  output: {
    path: './dist/public',
    filename: 'bundle.js',
  },

  module: { loaders },
}
```

We are telling Webpack that the source code of the client application is inside the src folder and we want the output bundle to be generated in the dist folder.

We also set the module loaders using the previous object we created with babel-loader. Done as simple as it should be.

The server configuration is slightly different, but it should be very easy for you to follow and understand:

```
const server = {
  entry: './src/server.js',

  output: {
    path: './dist',
    filename: 'server.js',
  },

  module: { loaders },

  target: 'node',

  externals: [nodeExternals()],
}
```

As you can see, entry, output, and module are basically the same, except for the file names.

The new parameters are the target, where we specify node to tell Webpack to ignore all the built-in system packages of Node.js, such as `fs` and `externals`, where we use the library we imported earlier to tell Webpack to ignore the dependencies.

Last but not least, we have to export the configurations as an array:

```
module.exports = [client, server]
```

The configuration is done. We are now ready to write some code, and we will start from the React application, which we are more familiar with.

Let's create an `src` folder and an `app.js` file inside it.

The `app.js` should have the following content:

```
import React from 'react'

const App = () => <div>Hello React</div>

export default App
```

Nothing complex here: we import React, we create an `App` component, which renders the **Hello React** message, and we export it.

Let's now create a `client.js`, which is actually responsible for rendering the `App` inside the DOM:

```
import React from 'react'
import ReactDOM from 'react-dom'
import App from './app'

ReactDOM.render(<App />, document.getElementById('app'))
```

Again, this should sound familiar, since we import React, ReactDOM, and the `App` we created earlier, and we use ReactDOM to render it in a DOM element with the ID `app`.

Let's now move to the server.

The first thing to do is create a template.js file, which exports a function that we will use to return the markup of the page that our server will give back to the browser:

```
export default body => `
  <!DOCTYPE html>
  <html>
    <head>
```

```
        <meta charset="UTF-8">
    </head>
    <body>
      <div id="app">${body}</div>
      <script src="/bundle.js"></script>
    </body>
  </html> `
```

It should be pretty straightforward: the function accepts a body, which we will later see contains the React app, and it returns the skeleton of the page.

It is worth noting that we load the bundle on the client side even if the app is server-side rendered. In fact, the SSR is only half of the job that React does to render our application. We still want our application to be a client-side application with all the features we can use in the browser, such as event handlers, for example.

Now it is time to create server.js, which has more dependencies and is worth exploring in detail:

```
import express from 'express'
import React from 'react'
import ReactDOM from 'react-dom/server'
import App from './app'
import template from './template'
```

The first thing that we import is express, the library that allows us to easily create a web server with some routes, and which is also able to serve static files.

Secondly, we import React and ReactDOM to render our App, which we import as well. Notice the /server path in the import statement of ReactDOM. The last thing we import is the template we defined earlier.

Now we create an Express application:

```
const app = express()
```

We tell the application where our static assets are stored:

```
app.use(express.static('dist/public'))
```

As you may have noticed, the path is the same that we used in the client configuration of Webpack as the output destination of the client bundle.

Then, here comes the logic of the SSR with React:

```
app.get('/', (req, res) => {
  const body = ReactDOM.renderToString(<App />)
  const html = template(body)
  res.send(html)
})
```

We are telling Express that we want to listen to the route, /, and when it gets hit by a client, we render the App to a string using the ReactDOM library. Here comes the magic and the simplicity of the server-side rendering of React.

What renderToString does is return a string representation of the DOM elements generated by our App component, the same tree that it would render in the DOM if we were using the ReactDOM render method.

The value of the body variable is something like the following:

```
<div data-reactroot="" data-reactid="1" data-react-
checksum="982061917">Hello React</div>
```

As you can see, it represents what we defined in the render method of our App, except for a couple of data attributes that React uses on the client to attach the client-side application to the server-side rendered string.

Now that we have the SSR representation of our app, we can use the template function to apply it to the HTML template and send it back to the browser within the Express response.

Last but not least, we have to start the Express application:

```
app.listen(3000, () => {
  console.log('Listening on port 3000')
})
```

We are now ready to go: there are only a few operations left.

The first one is defining the start script of npm and setting it to run the node server:

```
"scripts": {
  "build": "webpack",
  "start": "node ./dist/server"
},
```

The scripts are ready, so we can first build the application with the following:

```
npm run build
```

When the bundles are created we can run the following command:

```
npm start
```

Point the browser to `http://localhost:3000` and see the result.

There are two important things to note here: if we use the **View Page Source** feature of the browser, we can see the source code of the application being rendered and returned from the server, which we would not see if the SSR were not enabled.

Second, if we open DevTools and we have the React extension installed, we can see that the `App` component has been booted on the client as well.

The following screenshot shows the source of the page:

A data fetching example

The example in the previous section should explain clearly how to set up a Universal application in React.

It is pretty straightforward, and the main focus is on getting things done with regard to its configuration.

However, in a real-world application, we will likely want to load some data instead of a static React component such as the App in the example. Suppose we want to load *Dan Abramov*'s gists on the server and return the list of items from the Express app we just created.

In the data fetching examples in Chapter 5, *Proper Data Fetching*, we looked at how we can use componentDidMount to fire the data loading. That wouldn't work on the server because components do not get mounted on the DOM and the lifecycle hook never gets fired.

Using hooks that are executed earlier, such as componentWillMount, will not work either, because the data fetching operation is **async** while the renderToString is not. For that reason, we have to find a way to load the data beforehand and pass it to the component as props.

Let's look at how we can take the application from the previous section and change it a bit to make it load the gists during the server-side rendering phase.

The first thing to do is to change app.js to accept a list of gists as a prop, and loop through it in the render method to display their descriptions:

```
const App = ({ gists }) => (
  <ul>
    {gists.map(gist => (
      <li key={gist.id}>{gist.description}</li>
    ))}
  </ul>
)

App.propTypes = {
  gists: React.PropTypes.array,
}
```

Applying the concept that we learned in the previous chapter, we define a stateless functional component, which receives gists as a prop and loops through the elements to render a list of items.

Now we have to change the server to retrieve the `gists` and pass them to the component.

To use the **fetch** API on the server-side, we have to install a library called `isomorphic-fetch`, which implements the fetch standards. It can be used in Node.js and the browser:

```
npm install --save isomorphic-fetch
```

We first import the library in our `server.js`:

```
import fetch from 'isomorphic-fetch'
```

The API call we want to make looks as follows:

```
fetch('https://api.github.com/users/gaearon/gists')
  .then(response => response.json())
  .then(gists => {

  })
```

Here, the `gists` are available to be used inside the last then function. In our case we want to pass them down to the `App`.

So, we can change the `/` route as follows:

```
app.get('/', (req, res) => {
  fetch('https://api.github.com/users/gaearon/gists')
    .then(response => response.json())
    .then(gists => {
      const body = ReactDOM.renderToString(<App gists={gists} />)
      const html = template(body)

      res.send(html)
    })
})
```

Here, we first fetch the `gists` and then we render the `App` to a string, passing the property.

Once the `App` is rendered and we have its markup, we use the template we used in the previous section and we return it to the browser.

Run the following command in the console and point the browser to `http://localhost:3000`. You should be able to see a server-side render list of `gists`:

```
npm run build && npm start
```

To make sure that the list is rendered from the Express app you can navigate here:

```
view-source:http://localhost:3000/
```

You will see the markup and the descriptions of the `gists`.

That is great, and it looks easy, but if we check the DevTools console we can see the following error:

> **Cannot read property 'map' of undefined**

The reason we see the error is that, on the client, we are rendering the App again but without passing any `gists` to it.

This could sound counter-intuitive in the beginning because we might think that React is smart enough to use the gists rendered within the server-side string on the client. But that is not what happens, so we have to find a way to make the gists available on the client side as well.

You may consider that you can execute the fetch again on the client. That would work, but it is not optimal because you would end up firing two HTTP calls, one on the Express server and one in the browser.

If we think about it, we already made the call on the server and we have all the data we need. A typical solution to share data between the server and the client, is dehydrating the data in the HTML markup and hydrating it back in the browser.

This seems like a complex concept, but it is not. We will look at how easy it is to implement now.

The first thing we must do is to inject the gists in the template after we fetched them on the client. To do this, we have to change the template a bit:

```
export default (body, gists) => `
  <!DOCTYPE html>
  <html>
    <head>
      <meta charset="UTF-8">
    </head>
    <body>
      <div id="app">${body}</div>
      <script>window.gists = ${JSON.stringify(gists)}</script>
      <script src="/bundle.js"></script>
    </body>
  </html>
`
```

The template function now accepts two parameters: the body of the app and the collection of gists.

The first one is inserted inside the app element, while the second is used to define a global gists variable attached to window, so that we can use it in the client.

Inside the Express route, we just have to change the line where we generate the template passing the body, as follows:

```
const html = template(body, gists)
```

Last but not least, we have to use the gists attached to window inside the client.js, which is pretty easy:

```
ReactDOM.render(
  <App gists={window.gists} />,
  document.getElementById('app')
)
```

We read the gists directly and we pass them to the App component that gets rendered on the client.

Now run the following again:

```
npm run build && npm start
```

If we point the browser window to http://localhost:3000, the error is gone, and if we inspect the App component using React DevTools, we can see how the client-side App component receives the collection of gists.

Next.js

You have looked at the basics of server-side rendering with React and you can use the project we created as a starting point for a real app.

However, you may think that there is too much boilerplate and that you are required to know too many different tools to run a simple Universal application with React.

This is a common feeling, called **JavaScript Fatigue**, as described in the introduction to this book.

Luckily, Facebook developers and other companies in the React community are working very hard to improve the DX and make the life of developers easier. You should have used `create-react-app` at this point to try out the examples in the previous chapters, and you should understand how it makes it very simple to create and run React applications without requiring developers to learn many technologies and tools.

Now, `create-react-app` does not support SSR yet, but there's a company called *Zeit* who created a tool called **Next.js**, which makes it incredibly easy to generate Universal applications without worrying about configuration files. It also reduces the boilerplate a lot.

It is important to say that using abstractions is always very good for building applications quickly. However, it is crucial to know how the internals work before adding too many layers, and that is why we started with the manual process before learning Next.js.

We have looked at how SSR works and how we can pass the state from the server to the client. Now that the base concepts are clear, we can move to a tool that hides a little bit of complexity and makes us write less code to achieve the same results.

We will create the same app where all the gists from *Dan Abramov* are loaded, and you will see how clean and simple the code is thanks to Next.js.

First of all, let's move into an empty folder and create a new project:

```
npm init
```

When this is done, we can install the library:

```
npm install --save next
```

Now that the project is created, we just have to add an npm script to run the binary:

```
"scripts": {
  "dev": "next"
},
```

Perfect, it is now time to generate our App component.

Next.js is based on conventions, with the most important one being that you can create pages to match the browser URLs. The default page is index, so we can create a folder called pages and put an `index.js` file inside it.

We start importing the dependencies:

```
import React from 'react'
import fetch from 'isomorphic-fetch'
```

Again, we import `isomorphic-fetch` because we want to be able to use the fetch function on the server-side.

We then define a class called app, which inherits from `React.Component`:

```
class App extends React.Component
```

Inside the class, we define a **static async** function, called `getInitialProps`, which is where we tell Next.js which data we want to load, both on the server and on the client. The library will make the object returned from the function available as props inside the component.

The keywords `static` and `async` applied to a class method mean that the function can be accessed outside the instance of the class and that the function yields the execution of the wait instructions inside its body.

These concepts are pretty advanced, and they are not part of the scope of this chapter, but if you are interested in them, you should check out the ECMAScript proposals.

The implementation of the method we just described is as follows:

```
static async getInitialProps() {
  const url = 'https://api.github.com/users/gaearon/gists'
  const response = await fetch(url)
  const gists = await response.json()

  return { gists }
}
```

We are telling the function to fire the fetch and wait for the response; then we are transforming the response into JSON, which returns a promise. When the promise is resolved, we are able to return the props object with the gists.

The render method of the component looks pretty similar to the preceding one:

```
render() {
  return (
    <ul>
      {this.props.gists.map(gist => (
        <li key={gist.id}>{gist.description}</li>
      ))}
    </ul>
  )
}
```

However, it uses `this.props.gists` because we are inside a class instance.

Finally, we define the `PropTypes`, as you should always do when creating components:

```
App.propTypes = {
  gists: React.PropTypes.array,
}
```

Then we export the component:

```
export default App
```

Now open the console and run the following:

```
npm run dev
```

We will see the following output:

```
> Ready on http://localhost:3000
```

If we point the browser to that URL, we can see the Universal application in action.

It is really impressive how easy it is to set up a Universal application with a few lines of code and zero configuration, thanks to Next.js.

You may also notice that, if you edit the application inside your editor, you will be able to see the results within the browser instantly without needing to refresh the page. That is another feature of Next.js, which enables hot module replacement. It is incredibly useful in development mode.

If you liked this chapter, go and give them a star on GitHub:

```
https://github.com/zeit/next.js
```

Summary

The journey through server-side rendering has come to an end. You are now able to create a server-side rendered application with React, and it should be clear why it can be useful for you. SEO is certainly one of the main reasons, but social sharing and performance are important factors as well.

You learned how it is possible to load the data on the server and dehydrate it in the HTML template to make it available for the client-side application when it boots on the browser.

Finally, you have looked at how tools such as Next.js can help you reduce the boilerplate and hide some of the complexity that setting up a server-side render React application usually brings to the code base.

In the next chapter, we will talk about performance.

9
Improve the Performance of Your Applications

The effective performance of a web application is critical to providing a good user experience and improving conversions. The React library implements different techniques to render our components fast and to touch the DOM as little as possible. Applying changes to the DOM is usually expensive and so minimizing the number of operations is crucial.

However, there are some particular scenarios where React cannot optimize the process and it's up to the developer implementing specific solutions to make the application run smoothly.

In this chapter, we will go through the basic concepts of performance of React and we will learn how to use some APIs to help the library find the optimal path to update the DOM without degrading the user experience. We will also see some common mistakes that can harm our applications and make them slower.

Through the simple examples in this chapter, you will learn about the tools that we can import into our codebase to monitor performance and find bottlenecks. We will also see how immutability and the `PureComponent` are the perfect tools to build fast React applications.

We should avoid optimizing our components for the sake of it and it is important to apply the techniques that we will see in the following sections only when they are needed.

In this chapter we will see the following:

- How reconciliation works and how we can help React do a better job using the keys
- How using the production version of React makes the library faster

- What shouldComponentUpdate and PureComponent can do for us and how to use them
- Common optimization techniques and common performance-related mistakes
- What it means to use immutable data and how to do it
- Useful tools and libraries to make our applications run faster

Reconciliation and keys

Most of the time, React is fast enough by default and you do not need to do anything more to improve the performance of your application. React utilizes different techniques to optimize the rendering of the components on the screen.

When React has to display a component, it calls its **render method** and the render methods of its children recursively. The render method of a component returns a tree of React elements, which React uses to decide which DOM operations have to be done to update the UI.

Whenever a component's state changes, React calls the render methods on the nodes again and it compares the result with the previous tree of React elements. The library is smart enough to figure out the minimum set of operations required to apply the expected changes on the screen. This process is called **reconciliation** and it is managed transparently by React. Thanks to that, we can easily describe how our components have to look at a given point in time in a declarative way and let the library do the rest.

React tries to apply the smallest possible number of operations on the DOM because touching the **Document Object Model** is an expensive operation.

However, comparing two trees of elements is not free either and React makes two assumptions to reduce its complexity:

- If two elements have a different type, they render a different tree
- Developers can use keys to mark children as stable across different render calls

The second point is interesting from a developer perspective because it gives us a tool to help React render our views faster.

We will now go through a simple example which will make it clear how using keys in the proper way could make a significant difference.

Let's start by creating a simple component that displays a list of items and a button that appends a new item to the list causing a new render of the component.

We use a class here because we want to store the current list inside the state and we also need an event handler for when the button is clicked:

```
class List extends React.Component
```

The `List` component has a constructor where we initialize the list and we bind the event handler:

```
constructor(props) {
  super(props)

  this.state = {
    items: ['foo', 'bar'],
  }

  this.handleClick = this.handleClick.bind(this)
}
```

We then define the event handler that appends a new item to the list and stores the resulting array into the state:

```
handleClick() {
  this.setState({
    items: this.state.items.concat('baz'),
  })
}
```

Finally, we specify the `render` method where we loop through the items displaying every single element of the list and declaring the `button` with its `onClick` event handler:

```
render() {
  return (
    <div>
      <ul>
        {this.state.items.map(item => <li>{item}</li>)}
      </ul>
      <button onClick={this.handleClick}>+</button>
    </div>
  )
}
```

The component is ready and if you add it to your application (or if you create a new application using `create-react-app` to try it), you will see that the **foo** and **bar** items are shown on the screen and that clicking the + button adds **baz** at the end of the list.

That is how we expect it to work but, to have a clear idea of what React is doing, we need to install a new tool which helps us store and display performance-related information. The tool is a React **add-on** which can be easily installed with:

```
npm install --save-dev react-addons-perf
```

Once it is installed we can import it inside the `List` component file that we created earlier:

```
import Perf from 'react-addons-perf'
```

The `Perf` object has some useful methods that we can be used to monitor the performance of our React components. Using `start()`, we begin storing the information and with `stop()` we tell the add-on that we have enough data and we are ready to display it.

There are different methods which can be used to display the information we've previously gathered in the browser console. The most useful one is `printWasted` which prints out the time that the components have spent executing their render methods and returning the same elements as the previous execution. The `Perf` add-on also gives us some interesting information relating to the React operations in the DOM and it is this function that we are going to use to verify how crucial keys are to the improvement of our application's performance. The method is called `printOperations` and we call it as soon as the component has been updated to display the DOM operations that have been applied in the browser. To start and stop tracking and display the results, we can simply use two lifecycle hooks that React provides.

The first method that we are going to implement is `componentWillUpdate`, which is fired right before the component is updated and re-rendered:

```
componentWillUpdate() {
  Perf.start()
}
```

Inside this lifecycle hook we start monitoring the perf, using the `Perf` add-on's `start()` function. As soon as the update is done, we stop tracking and we do so in the `componentDidUpdate` hook, as follows:

```
componentDidUpdate() {
  Perf.stop()
  Perf.printOperations()
}
```

As you can see, here we stop measuring and we also fire the `printOperations` method of the `Perf` add-on to see which operations React has made on the DOM to add the **baz** element on the screen.

If we run the component and click the **+** button, we can see the operations are listed in a table in the DevTools console. The relevant columns are Operation, which shows: `"insert child"` and Payload, which shows: `"{"toIndex":2,"content":"LI"}"`.

React has figured out that the change needed to append a child at the end of the current list is to insert a new `LI` element as a child to the existing list at the index number two (third element).

As you may notice, instead of repainting everything on the screen, React calculated the minimum amount of operations needed to update the DOM. This is great and it is more than enough for the majority of the use cases.

However, there are some particular scenarios where React is not smart enough to figure out the best path to follow and we have to help it using the keys. If we change the example above a little bit, in particular the event handler, and instead of appending **baz** at the end of the list we insert it as a first element, we can see how React behaves in a non-optimal way.

To put an element as the first item of an array we can use JavaScript's `unshift` and apply it to a copy of the array that is stored in the current state. We have to operate on a copy of the array because the `unshift` method does not return a new array but it mutates the original one, which is something we should avoid when working with the state. The new `onClick` handler is the following one:

```
handleClick() {
  const items = this.state.items.slice()
  items.unshift('baz')

  this.setState({
    items,
  })
}
```

Where we simply clone the array, we insert the **baz** item on top and we set it back to the state, causing a re-rendering.

If we run the `List` component, we see the initial list items on the screen, **foo** and **bar**, and when we click **+**, the new **baz** item is added as a first element.

Everything works as expected but if we look inside the browser DevTools again we notice that React has done multiple operations. Again the Operations and Payload columns are the most interesting ones and we can see that React has applied three changes:

- It has replaced the text of the first item with **baz**, the new value
- It has replaced the text of the second item with **foo**, the value of the former first item
- It has inserted a new child at index 2, at the bottom of the list

React, instead of just adding the new element at the top of the list and shifting the other ones down, has changed the values of the previous ones and added a new item at the end of the list.

React does this because it just checks the equality of the children and, if it finds that the first one is different, it changes all the items of the list as if they were new.

In this small example, this does not create any visible performance issue but, if you think about a real-world application with hundreds of elements, this could become a major problem.

Luckily, React gives us a tool called **key** which we can use to help the library figure out which elements are changed and which ones have been added or removed.

Using key is simple, we have to add a unique key attribute to each one of the items in the list. It is important for the value of the key attribute not to change on each render, because React will compare it with its previous value to decide if the element is new or if it is an existing one.

For example, we can change the render method of the List component in the following way:

```
render() {
  return (
    <div>
      <ul>
        {this.state.items.map(item => <li key={item}>{item}</li>)}
      </ul>
      <button onClick={this.handleClick}>+</button>
    </div>
  )
}
```

When we set the key of each list item to the value of the item itself and we run the component again in the browser, we see that the behavior is not changed: we first see a list of two items and then the new item is added above it when the button is clicked.

However, if we open the DevTools browser we can see that the `Perf` add-on has logged something different from the previous execution.

In fact, the operation says that a single element has been inserted and, most importantly, the payload says that the element has been inserted at position 0, the first position.

That is great: using the keys, we helped React to determine the minimum set of operations and improved the rendering performance of our components. With this simple rule in mind, we can cover many instances where we might harm the performance if we did not use the keys.

It is important to say that it is easy for us to remember this rule because, it provides a warning in the browser console, every time we forget to add the keys:

> **Each child in an array or iterator should have a unique "key" prop. Check the render method of `List`.**

This error message is particularly useful because it also gives us information on which component we have to modify to fix the issue.

Also, if you use **Eslint,** as we saw in the `Chapter 2`, *Clean Up Your Code*, and you enabled the `jsx-key` rule of the `eslint-plugin-react`, the linter will complain if the keys are missing.

Optimization techniques

It is important to notice that, in all the examples in this book, we are using apps that have either been created with `create-react-app` or have been created from scratch, but always with the development version of React.

Using the development version of React is very useful for coding and debugging as it gives you all the necessary information to fix the various issues. However, all the checks and warnings come with a cost which we want to avoid in production.

So, the very first optimization that we should do to our applications is to build the bundle setting the `NODE_ENV` environment variable to `production`. This is pretty easy with **Webpack** and it is just a matter of using the `DefinePlugin` in the following way:

```
new webpack.DefinePlugin({
  'process.env': {
    NODE_ENV: JSON.stringify('production')
  }
}),
```

To achieve the best performance, we not only want to create the bundle with the production flag activated but we also want to minify the resulting code to save bytes and make the application load faster. To do so, we can easily add the following plugin to the list of plugins in the **Webpack** configuration:

```
new webpack.optimize.UglifyJsPlugin()
```

If we run the production version of React and we realize that some parts of our applications are still slow, there are different techniques that we can put in place to improve the rendering of our components.

It is important to say that we should never optimize an application before having measured its performance and understood where the bottlenecks are. Premature optimizations often lead to unnecessary complexity, which is something we should avoid as much as we can.

It also worth saying again that React already implements some techniques to make our applications quicker and smoother and so most of the time we do not need anything more than this.

However, there are some particular cases where the optimizations are not enough and we want to help the library to give us the best possible experience. In those cases, we can tell React to avoid reconciling some parts of the tree.

Should component update

For many developers, the way the reconciler algorithm works is confusing. They often think that, since React is smart enough to find out the shortest path to apply the changes to the DOM, the render method of the components that are not changed does not ever get called. That's unfortunately far from being true.

In fact, to find out the necessary steps to reduce the DOM operations, React, has to fire the render methods of all the components and compare the results with the previous ones.

If nothing changes, no changes will be made in the DOM, which is great. But if our render methods do complex operations, React will take some time to figure out that no operations have to be done, which is not optimal.

We surely want our components to be simple and we should avoid doing expensive operations inside the renderer. However, sometimes we simply cannot manage this and our applications become slow, even if the DOM is not touched at all.

React is not able to figure out which components do not need to be updated but we have a function that we can implement to tell the library when to update a component or not.

The method is called `shouldComponentUpdate` and if it returns `false`, the component and all its children's render methods are not called during an update of its parents.

For example, if you try to add the following code to the previously created list:

```
shouldComponentUpdate() {
  return false
}
```

You can see that clicking on the + button has no effect whatsoever on the application inside the browser, even though the state changes. That is because we are telling React that the component does not need to be updated.

Returning `false` all the time is far from useful and so developers usually check if the props or the state are changed inside that method.

In the case of the `List`, for example, we should check if the items array has been modified or not, and return a value accordingly.

The `shouldComponentUpdate` method passes two parameters which we can use to implement those checks: the first parameter represents the `nextProps` while the second parameter represents the `nextState`.

In our case, we could do something like this:

```
shouldComponentUpdate(nextProps, nextState) {
  return this.state.items !== nextState.items
}
```

We return `true` only if the items are changed, while we stop the rendering in any other case. Suppose, for example, that our `List` is a child of a component that gets updated frequently but its state does not affect the `List` in any way: We can use `shoudlComponentUpdate` to tell React to stop running the render methods from that component to its children.

Checking if all the props and all the state attributes are changed is a boring job and it is sometimes hard to maintain complex `shouldComponentUpdate` implementations, especially when the requirements change frequently.

For that reason, React gives us a special component from which we can inherit and which implements a shallow comparison of all the props and the state attributes for us.

Using it is pretty straightforward, we just have to extend `React.PureComponent` instead of `React.Component` when we create our component classes.

It is important to notice that the shallow comparison, as the name suggests, does not check for deep and nested properties in objects and it can sometimes give unexpected results.

It works very well with immutable data structures, which we will see in more detail later in this chapter. It is worth saying that performing a deep comparison of complex objects can sometimes be more expensive than the render method itself.

That is why the `PureComponent` should be used only when it is needed and only once the performance have been measured and you have figured out which components are taking too much time to be executed.

Stateless functional components

Another concept that is sometimes counter-intuitive for beginners is the fact that stateless components do not give us any benefits regarding performance.

They are great for the many reasons that we saw in Chapter 3, *Create Truly Reusable Components*, and for the way they make our applications simpler and easier to reason about but they do not have (yet) any internal implementation that makes them faster.

It is easy to think that they are rendered quicker because they do not have an instance, and do not have a state or event handlers, but at the moment that's not the case.

In the future, they might be optimized (according to the React team) but today they perform even worse because it is not possible to use the `shouldComponentUpdate` method which as we have seen before, can help React render the tree faster.

Common solutions

We have seen how using the `PureComponent` can help us to tell React when a **subtree** has to be rendered or not. If utilized in the right way, it could improve the performance of our applications a lot. It is also important to stress that is should be used only after the application has been monitored and the bottleneck has been found.

There are some tricky situations where extending the `PureComponent` does not give the expected results; usually, the cause is that our props or state attributes are changing even if we think they are not. Sometimes it is not easy to figure out which props are causing the component to re-render or we do not know which components can be optimized with the `PureComponent`.

Most of the time, refactoring the components and putting the state in the right place can greatly assist the optimization of the application.

In this section, we will look at some common tools and solutions to solve re-rendering issues, figuring out which components can be optimized. We will also look at how to refactor complex component into small ones to achieve better performance.

Why did you update?

There are different things we can do to find out which components do not need to be updated. One of the easiest is to install a third-party library that can provide the information automatically.

First of all, we have to type the following command in the terminal:

```
npm install --save-dev why-did-you-update
```

And add the following snippet after the `import` statement of React:

```
if (process.env.NODE_ENV !== 'production') {
  const { whyDidYouUpdate } = require('why-did-you-update')
  whyDidYouUpdate(React)
}
```

We are basically saying that, in development mode, we want to load the library and patch React using the `whyDidYouUpdate` method. It is important to say that this library should not be enabled in production.

If we now go back to the `List` example of the previous section and we change it a little bit, we can see the library in action.

The first thing we have to do is to modify the `render` method as follows:

```
render() {
  return (
    <div>
      <ul>
        {this.state.items.map(item => (
```

```
          <Item key={item} item={item} />
        ))}
      </ul>
      <button onClick={this.handleClick}>+</button>
    </div>
  )
}
```

Instead of rendering the single list items inside the map function, we return a custom Item component to which we pass the current item and we use the key to tell React which components existed before the update.

We can now implement the item component, extending React.Component:

```
class Item extends React.Component
```

At the moment it only implements the render method, which does what we were doing inside the render method of the List:

```
render() {
  return (
    <li>{this.props.item}</li>
  )
}
```

Before running it in the browser, we may also want to change the method of the Perf add-on because, in this case, we are more interested in the time wasted rendering unchanged components, rather than the DOM operations that have been executed:

```
componentDidUpdate() {
  Perf.stop()
  Perf.printWasted()
}
```

Nice! If we now render the component inside the browser, we can see the **foo** and **bar** items and if we press the + button we see two things happening inside the DevTools console.

The first one is the output from the whyDidYouUpdate function which tells us that we can avoid re-rendering some components:

```
Item.props
  Value did not change. Avoidable re-render!
  before Object {item: "foo"}
  after  Object {item: "foo"}
Item.props
  Value did not change. Avoidable re-render!
  before Object {item: "bar"}
```

```
after    Object {item: "bar"}
```

In fact, even if React does not touch the DOM for the **foo** and **bar** items, their render methods are still being called with the same props, which makes React perform an additional job. This is very useful information that is sometimes not easy to find.

After those lines, we can see the output of the `Perf` add-on which measures the time we are wasting firing the render method of the `Item` components when the props are unchanged.

Now, we can easily fix the issue by modifying the extends statement of the Item component from `extends React.Component` to:

```
class Item extends React.PureComponent
```

If we now open the browser and run the application again, clicking the + button we see that nothing is logged into the console which means that we are not rendering any `Item` for which the props are not changed.

Regarding perceived performance, there is not much difference in this small example, but if you imagine a big application that shows hundreds of list items, this small change can represent a huge win.

Creating functions inside the render method

Now, let's keep on adding features to the `List` as we would do in a real-world application and see whether, at some point, we manage to break the benefits given by the `PureComponent`.

For example, we want to add a click event handler on each item so that, if the item gets clicked, we log its value into the console.

This is far from being a useful feature in a real application but you can easily figure out how, with a small amount of effort, you can create some more complex operations like, for example, showing a new window with the item's data.

To add the logging feature we have to apply two changes, one to the `render` method of the `List` and the other one to the `render` method of the `Item`.

Let's start with the first one:

```
render() {
  return (
    <div>
      <ul>
        {this.state.items.map(item => (
          <Item
            key={item}
            item={item}
            onClick={() => console.log(item)}
          />
        ))}
      </ul>
      <button onClick={this.handleClick}>+</button>
    </div>
  )
}
```

We added a `onClick` prop to the `Item` component and we set it to a function that, when called, logs the current item into the console.

To make it work, we have to add the logic on the `Item` components as well, and we can just use the `onClick` prop as the `onClick` handler of the `<li>` element:

```
render() {
  return (
    <li onClick={this.props.onClick}>
      {this.props.item}
    </li>
  )
}
```

The component is still pure and we expect it to not re-render when the values have not changed when **baz** is added to the list.

Unfortunately, if we run the component in the browser, we notice some new logs in DevTools: first of all, the `whyDidYouUpdate` library is telling us that there is a possibly avoidable re-render because the `onClick` function is always the same:

```
Item.props.onClick
  Value is a function. Possibly avoidable re-render?
  before onClick() {
    return console.log(item);
  }
  after  onClick() {
    return console.log(item);
```

```
    }
  Item.props.onClick
    Value is a function. Possibly avoidable re-render?
    before onClick() {
      return console.log(item);
    }
    after  onClick() {
      return console.log(item);
    }
```

Secondly, we can see that the `Perf` add-on is informing us that we are wasting some time rendering the `List > Item` component.

The reason React thinks that we are passing a new function on every render is because the arrow function returns a newly created function every time it is invoked, even if the implementation remains the same. This is a pretty common mistake when using React and it can be easily fixed by refactoring the components a bit.

Unfortunately, we cannot define the logging function once in the parent because we need to know which child has fired it; so that is why creating it inside the loop could seem the best solution.

What we actually have to do is move part of the logic inside the item that knows the item that has been clicked.

Let's see the full implementation of the `Item`, which extends the `PureComponent`:

```
class Item extends React.PureComponent
```

It has a `constructor` where we bind the click handler which is now part of its implementation:

```
constructor(props) {
  super(props)

  this.handleClick = this.handleClick.bind(this)
}
```

Inside the `handleClick` function we call the `onClick` handler that we received from the `props` passing the current item which has been clicked within the `<li>` element:

```
handleClick() {
  this.props.onClick(this.props.item)
}
```

Finally, in the `render` method we use the new local event handler:

```
render() {
  return (
    <li onClick={this.handleClick}>
      {this.props.item}
    </li>
  )
}
```

The last thing to do is change the `List` component's render to make it not return a new function at every single render, as follows:

```
render() {
  return (
    <div>
      <ul>
        {this.state.items.map(item => (
          <Item key={item} item={item} onClick={console.log} />
        ))}
      </ul>
      <button onClick={this.handleClick}>+</button>
    </div>
  )
}
```

As you can see, we are passing the function we wanted to use, in this case `console.log`, which will be called inside the children with the right parameter. Doing so, the instance of the function in the `List` is always the same and it does not fire any re-rendering.

If we now run the component in the browser and we click the + button to add the new item, which causes the `List` component to render, we can see that we are not wasting time anymore.

Also, if we click on any items in the list we will see its value in the console as well.

As *Dan Abramov* says, it is not a problem by itself to use arrow functions inside the render method (or even to use bind to avoid binding in the constructor), we just have to be careful and make sure that it does not force any unnecessary re-rendering when the `PureComponent` is in action.

Constants props

Let's keep on improving our list example and see what happens when we add new features.

In this case, we will learn how to avoid a common error when using the `PureComponent`, which makes it less effective.

Suppose we want to add a prop to our `Item` component which represents a list of statuses that the item can have. There are many ways of implementing it, but our focus is more on the way we pass down the default values.

If we change the `render` method of the `List` component as follows:

```
render() {
  return (
    <div>
      <ul>
        {this.state.items.map(item => (
          <Item
            key={item}
            item={item}
            onClick={console.log}
            statuses={['open', 'close']}
          />
        ))}
      </ul>
      <button onClick={this.handleClick}>+</button>
    </div>
  )
}
```

In the preceding code, for each `Item`, we set the `key` and the `item` prop to the current value of the `item`. We fire `console.log` when the `onClick` event is fired inside the `Item` and we now have a new prop which represents the possible statuses of the `item`.

Now, if we render the `List` component inside the browser we see **foo** and **bar** as usual and if we click the **+** button to add **baz** we notice a new message in the console:

```
Item.props.statuses
  Value did not change. Avoidable re-render!
  before ["open", "close"]
  after  ["open", "close"]
Item.props.statuses
  Value did not change. Avoidable re-render!
  before ["open", "close"]
  after  ["open", "close"]
```

The message is telling us that even if the values inside the array stay the same, on every render we are passing a new instance of the array to the `Item`.

The reason behind this behavior is that all the objects return a new instance when created and a new array is never equal to another, even if they contain the same values:

```
[] === []
false
```

There is also a table printed on the console, which shows the time that React is wasting rendering the items with unchanged props when there is no need to touch the DOM.

What we can do to solve the issue here is to create the array once, and always pass the same instance to every render.

Something like:

```
const statuses = ['open', 'close']
...
render() {
  return (
    <div>
      <ul>
        {this.state.items.map(item => (
          <Item
            key={item}
            item={item}
            onClick={console.log}
            statuses={statuses}
          />
        ))}
      </ul>
      <button onClick={this.handleClick}>+</button>
    </div>
  )
}
```

If we try the component again in the browser, we see that the console now contains no message, which means that the items do not re-render themselves unnecessarily when the new element is added.

Refactoring and good design

In the last part of this section, we will see how we can refactor an existing component (or design a new one in a better way) to improve the performance of our application.

Poor design choices often lead to issues and, in the case of React, if we do not put the state in the right place, the risk is that our components are going to render more than needed.

As we said before, this is not a huge problem if a component renders itself more often than necessary. The problem becomes a real one only when we measure performance and realize that rendering a long list of items many times makes the application less responsive.

The component that we are going to create is similar to the previous one, a to-do list-like component with a form to let the users enter a new item.

As usual, we will start with a basic version and we will optimize it step by step.

The component is called `Todos`, that is a class which `extends React.Component`:

```
class Todos extends React.Component
```

Inside the `constructor`, we initialize the state and bind the event handlers:

```
constructor(props) {
  super(props)

  this.state = {
    items: ['foo', 'bar'],
    value: '',
  }

  this.handleChange = this.handleChange.bind(this)
  this.handleClick = this.handleClick.bind(this)
}
```

The state has two attributes:

- **The items**: Which is the list of items with a couple of default values; and it's also the array where the new items will be added
- **The value**: Which is the current value of the input that the users can fill to add new items

You should be now able to infer the functionalities of the event handlers from their names. We have the `handleChange` which is fired every time a user types a character in the form:

```
handleChange({ target }) {
  this.setState({
    value: target.value,
  })
}
```

As we saw in Chapter 6, *Write Code for the Browser,* the `onChange` handler receives the event which has a target property that represents the input element and we store its value inside the state to control the component.

Then there is the `handleClick` which is fired when the users submit the form to add a new item:

```
handleClick() {
  const items = this.state.items.slice()
  items.unshift(this.state.value)

  this.setState({
    items,
  })
}
```

The click handler is pretty similar to the previous one except that it uses the value from the state instead of a constant string and it adds it as the first element on a copy of the current array.

Finally, we describe our view in the `render` method:

```
render() {
  return (
    <div>
      <ul>
        {this.state.items.map(item => <li key={item}>{item}</li>)}
      </ul>
      <div>
        <input
          type="text"
          value={this.state.value}
          onChange={this.handleChange}
        />
        <button onClick={this.handleClick}>+</button>
      </div>
    </div>
  )
```

```
}
```

We have the unordered list, where we loop through the items collection and we print every single item inside a `<li>` element. Then there is the controlled input field and we set its current values as well as listen to the change event. Last but not least, there is a + button which we use to submit the value and add it to the array of items.

Here is a screenshot of the component in action:

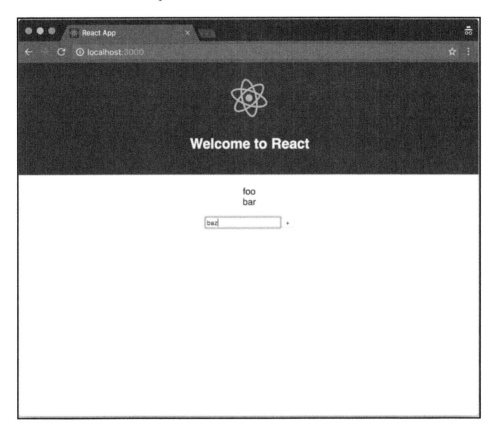

Now, this component works and, if we run it inside the browser, we'll see the list of items with the two default values and the form which we can use to add new items to the list. As soon as we click on the button, the new item is added to the top of the list.

There are no particular problems with this component, unless we start adding hundreds of items. At that point, we realize that typing into the field becomes laggy. The reason for the reduction in performance as soon as the number of items grows is that the list re-renders every time a user types in the field. When we update the state with the new value of the controlled component, in fact, React calls the render again to see if the elements are different.

The only change is the value of the `input` element and that is going to be the only mutation applied to the DOM; but, to figure out what operations are needed, React has to render the entire component and all its children and rendering a big list of items many times over is expensive.

Now, if we look at the state object of the component it's pretty clear that it is not well structured. In fact, we are storing the items as well as the value of the form field which are two entirely different things.

Our goal is always to have components that do one thing very well, rather than components with multiple purposes.

The solution here is to split the component into smaller ones, each one with a clear responsibility and state.

We need a common parent, because the components are related. In fact, if we don't want to re-render the list every time a user types in the field, we also do not want to render the list again as soon as the form is submitted and the new item is added.

To do so, we change the `Todos` component to store only the list of items, which is the part of the store that is shared between the list and the form.

Then we create a separate list which only receives the items and a form which has its state for controlling the input field. The field fires a callback on the common parent to update the list when the form is submitted.

Let's start changing the `Todos` component:

```
class Todos extends React.Component
```

In the constructor, we now define only the default items inside the state and we bind a single submit handler which is the callback of the `Form` component:

```
constructor(props) {
  super(props)

  this.state = {
    items: ['foo', 'bar'],
```

```
    }

    this.handleSubmit = this.handleSubmit.bind(this)
  }
```

The implementation of the submit handler is the same as we've seen before on the click handler:

```
handleSubmit(value) {
  const items = this.state.items.slice()
  items.unshift(value)

  this.setState({
    items,
  })
}
```

Except that it receives the value of the new item as a parameter of the callback. It then clones the array and adds the value as its first element. When the array is updated, it gets added back to the state.

The render method is much cleaner now, because we just render two custom components, each one with their props:

```
render() {
  return (
    <div>
      <List items={this.state.items} />
      <Form onSubmit={this.handleSubmit} />
    </div>
  )
}
```

The List component receives the items from the state, and the Form receives the handleSubmit function as a callback and it fires the onSubmit when the user clicks the + button.

It is now time to create the subcomponents, and we will start from the List just by extracting the part of the code from the previous render method.

The List can be implemented as a class and it inherits from the PureComponent so that it gets re-rendered only when the items are changed:

```
class List extends React.PureComponent
```

The `render` method is pretty simple and it just loops through the items in the array to generate the list:

```
render() {
  return (
    <ul>
      {this.props.items.map(item => <li key={item}>{item}</li>)}
    </ul>
  )
}
```

Then, we have the `Form` component which is a bit more complex because it handles the state of the controlled input element. It extends the `PureComponent` as well so that it never gets re-rendered from the parent since the callback never changes:

```
class Form extends React.PureComponent
```

We define a constructor where we set the initial state and bind the change handler for the controlled input:

```
constructor(props) {
  super(props)

  this.state = {
    value: '',
  }

  this.handleChange = this.handleChange.bind(this)
}
```

The implementation of the change handler is very similar to any other controlled input we have seen until now:

```
handleChange({ target }) {
  this.setState({
    value: target.value,
  })
}
```

It receives the target element, which is our input, and saves its value into the state.

Finally, in the `render` method we declare the elements that compose our form:

```
render() {
  return (
    <div>
      <input
        type="text"
```

```
        value={this.state.value}
        onChange={this.handleChange}
      />
      <button
        onClick={() => this.props.onSubmit(this.state.value)}
      >+</button>
    </div>
  )
}
```

This includes the controlled input field where we set the value, and the change handler and the **+** button which fires the callback passing the current value. In this case, we can generate a function inside the `render` because there are no pure children.

Done! If we now run the newly created `Todos` component in the page, we see that the behavior is the same as before, but the list and the form have two separate states and they render only when their props change.

For example, if we try to add hundreds of items inside the list we see that the performance are not affected and the input field is not laggy. We've solved a performance issue just by refactoring the component and changing the design a bit by separating the responsibilities correctly.

Tools and libraries

In the next section, we will go through some techniques, tools, and libraries that we can apply to our codebase to monitor and improve the performance.

Immutability

As we have seen, the most powerful tool we can use to improve the performance of our React application is the `shouldComponentUpdate` using the `PureComponent`.

The only problem is that the `PureComponent` uses a shallow comparison method against the props and state, which means that if we pass an object as a prop and we mutate one of its values, we do not get the expected behavior.

In fact, a shallow comparison cannot find mutation on the properties and the components never get re-rendered, except when the object itself changes.

One way to solve this issue is using **immutable data**: Data that, once it gets created, cannot be mutated.

For example, we can set the state in the following mode:

```
const obj = this.state.obj
obj.foo = 'bar'
this.setState({ obj })
```

Even if the value of the `foo` attribute of the object is changed, the reference to the object is still the same and the shallow comparison does not recognize it.

What we can do instead is create a new instance every time we mutate the object, as follows:

```
const obj = Object.assign({}, this.state.obj, { foo: 'bar' })
this.setState({ obj })
```

In this case, we get a new object with the property `foo` set to `bar` and the shallow comparison would be able to find the difference.

With ES2015 and Babel there is another way to express the same concept in a more elegant way and it is by using the object spread operator:

```
const obj = { ...this.state.obj, foo: 'bar' }
this.setState({ obj })
```

This structure is more concise than the previous one and it produces the same result; but, at the time of writing, it requires the code to be transpiled to be executed inside the browser

React provides some immutability helpers to make it easy to work with immutable objects and there is also a popular library called `immutable.js` which has more powerful features but it requires to learn new APIs.

Monitoring tools

We have already seen how we can use the `Perf` add-on provided by React to track the performance of our components.

In our example, we started and stopped monitoring using the lifecycle hooks of the components, as follows:

```
componentWillUpdate() {
  Perf.start()
}
```

```
componentDidUpdate() {
  Perf.stop()
  Perf.printOperations()
}
```

After calling the stop method, we also used the `printOperations` function to print, in the browser console, the current DOM operation that React has made to apply the required changes.

This is great, and it is an incredibly useful tool. However using the hooks and polluting the codebase for tracking the component's performance can be overkill.

The best solution would be to be able to monitor the performance of components without modifying the code and to do that we can use the `chrome-react-perf` extension for Chrome.

It can be installed in the browser by following this URL:

`https://chrome.google.com/webstore/detail/reactperf/hacmcodfllhbnekmghgdlplbdna hmhmm`

The extension adds a panel in the DevTools which we can use to start and stop the `Perf` add-on in an easy and convenient way without writing any code.

Another tool which helps us easily collect information about our component's performance is `react-perf-tool` which is a component that we can install, import and add inside our application to get a nice interface to manage the `Perf` add-on within the browser window.

It renders a console at the bottom of the page from which we can start and stop monitoring. Instead of showing the data in the form of a table, it renders a beautiful graph which makes it simple to figure out the components that are taking more time than the others.

Babel plugins

There are also a couple of interesting **Babel** plugins that we can install and use to improve the performance of our React applications. They make the applications faster, optimizing parts of the code at build-time.

The first one is the **React constant elements transformer** which finds all the static elements that do not change depending on the props and extracts them from the render method (or the functional stateless components) to avoid calling `createElement` unnecessarily.

Using a Babel plugin is pretty straightforward, we first install it with npm:

```
npm install --save-dev babel-plugin-transform-react-constant-
elements
```

Then we edit our `.babelrc` file adding a `plugins` key with an array that has the value with the list of the plugin that we want to activate.

In this case, we have:

```
{
   "plugins": ["transform-react-constant-elements"]
}
```

The second Babel plugin we can choose to use to improve performance is the **React inline elements transform**, which replaces all the JSX declarations (or the `createElement` calls) with a more optimized version of them to make execution faster.

Install the plugin with:

```
npm install --save-dev babel-plugin-transform-react-inline-elements
```

Next, you can easily add the plugin to the array of plugin in the `.babelrc` file as follows:

```
{
   "plugins": ["transform-react-inline-elements"]
}
```

Both plugins should be used only in production because they make debugging harder in development mode.

Summary

Our journey through performance is finished and we can now optimize our applications to give users a better UX.

In this chapter, we learned how the reconciliation algorithm works and how React always tries to take the shortest path to apply changes to the DOM. We can also help the library to optimize its job by using the keys.

Always remember to use the production version of React when benchmarking with the `Perf` add-on to find the parts of your application that need optimization.

Once you've found your bottlenecks, you can apply one the techniques we have seen in this chapter to fix the issue. One of the first tools you can use is to extend the `PureComponent` and use immutable data to make your component re-render only when strictly needed.

Don't forget to avoid the common mistakes that make the `PureComponent` less effective, such as generating new functions inside the render method, or using constant as props.

We have learned how refactoring and designing your components structure in the proper way could provide a performance boost. Our goal is to have small components that do one single thing in the best possible way.

At the end of the chapter we talked about immutability and we've seen why it's important not to mutate data to make `shouldComponentUpdate` and the `shallowCompare` do their job. Finally, we ran through different tools and libraries that can make your applications faster.

In the next chapter, we'll look at testing and debugging.

10
About Testing and Debugging

React, thanks to components, makes it easy to test our applications. There are many different tools that we can use to create tests with React and we'll cover the most popular ones to understand the benefits they provide.

Jest is an all-in-one testing framework solution, maintained by *Christopher Pojer* from Facebook and contributors within the community, and aims to give you the best developer experience; but you can decide to create a custom setup with **Mocha** as well. We will look at both ways of building the best test environment.

You'll learn the difference between **Shallow rendering** and full DOM rendering with both **TestUtils** and **Enzyme**, how **Snapshot** Testing works, and how to collect some useful code coverage information.

Once the tools and their functionalities are well understood, we will cover a component from the Redux repository with tests and we'll look at some common testing solutions that can be applied in complex scenarios.

At the end of the chapter, you'll be able to create a test environment from scratch and write tests for your application's components.

In this chapter we will look at:

- Why it is important to test our applications, and how this help developers move faster
- How to set up a Jest environment to test components using the TestUtils
- How to set up the same environment with Mocha
- What Enzyme is and why it is a must-have for testing React applications
- How to test a real-world component
- The Jest snapshots and the Istanbul code coverage tools

- Common solutions for testing Higher-Order components and complex pages with multiple nested children
- The React developer tools and some error handling techniques

The benefits of testing

Testing web UIs has always been a hard job. From unit to end-to-end tests, the fact that the interfaces depend on browsers, user interactions, and many other variables makes it difficult to implement an effective testing strategy.

If you've ever tried to write end-to-end tests for the Web, you'll know how complex it is to get consistent results and how the results are often affected by false negatives due to different factors, such as the network. Other than that, user interfaces are frequently updated to improve experience, maximize conversions, or simply add new features.

If tests are hard to write and maintain, developers are less prone to cover their applications. On the other hand, tests are pretty important because they make developers more confident with their code, which is reflected in speed and quality. If a piece of code is well-tested (and tests are well-written) developers can be sure that it works and is ready to ship. Similarly, thanks to tests, it becomes easier to refactor the code because tests guarantee that the functionalities do not change during the rewrite.

Developers tend to focus on the feature they are currently implementing and sometimes it is hard to know if other parts of the application are affected by those changes. Tests help to avoid regressions because they can tell if the new code breaks the old tests. Greater confidence in writing new features leads to faster releases.

Testing the main functionalities of an application makes the codebase more solid and, whenever a new bug is found, it can be reproduced, fixed, and covered by tests so that it does not happen again in the future.

Luckily, React (and the component era), makes testing user interfaces easy and efficient. Testing components, or trees of components, is a less arduous job because every single part of the application has its responsibilities and boundaries.

If components are built in the right way, if they are pure and aim for composability and reusability, they can be tested as simple functions.

Another great power that modern tools bring to us the ability to run tests using Node and the console. Spinning up a browser for every single test makes tests slower and less predictable, degrading the developer experience; running the tests using the console instead is faster.

Testing components only in the console can sometimes give unexpected behaviors when they are rendered in a real browser but, in my experience, this is rare.

When we test React components we want to make sure that they work properly and that, given different sets of props, their output is always correct.

We may also want to cover all the various states that a component can have. The state might change by clicking a button so we write tests to check if all the event handlers are doing what they are supposed to do.

When all the functionalities of the component are covered but we want to do more, we can write tests to verify its behavior on **Edge cases**. Edge cases are states that the component can assume when, for example, all the props are null or there is an error. Once the tests are written, we can be pretty confident that the component behaves as expected.

Testing a single component is great, but it does not guarantee that multiple individually tested components will still work once they are put together. As we will see later, with React we can mount a tree of components and test the integration between them.

There are different techniques that we can use to write tests, and one of the most popular ones is **Test Driven Development (TDD)**. Applying TDD means writing the tests first and then writing the code to pass the tests.

Following this pattern helps us to write better code because we are forced to think more about the design before implementing the functionalities, which usually leads to higher quality.

Painless JavaScript testing with Jest

The most important way to learn how to test React components in the right way is by writing some code, and that is what we are going to do in this section.

The React documentation says that at Facebook they use Jest to test their components. However, React does not force you to use a particular test framework and you can use your favorite one without any problems.

In the next section, you will learn how it's possible to test components using Mocha.

To see Jest in action we are going to create a project from scratch, installing all the dependencies and writing a component with some tests. It'll be fun!

The first thing to do is to move into a new folder and run:

```
npm init
```

Once the `package.json` is created we can start installing the dependencies, with the first one being the `jest` package itself:

```
npm install --save-dev jest
```

To tell `npm` that we want to use the `jest` command to run the tests, we have to add the following scripts to the `package.json`:

```
"scripts": {
  "test": "jest"
},
```

In order to write components and tests using ES2015 and JSX, we have to install all Babel-related packages so that Jest can use them to transpile and understand the code.

The second set of dependencies is:

```
npm install --save-dev babel-jest babel-preset-es2015 babel-preset-
react
```

As you may know, we now have to create a `.babelrc` file, which is used by Babel to know the presets and the plugins that we would like to use inside the project.

`.babelrc` looks like the following:

```
{
  "presets": ["es2015", "react"]
}
```

Now it is time to install React and ReactDOM, which we need to create and render components:

```
npm install --save react react-dom
```

The setup is ready and we can run Jest against ES2015 code and render our components into the DOM, but there is one more thing to do.

As we said, we want to be able to run the tests with Node and the console. To do that we cannot render the components using ReactDOM, because it needs the browser's DOM.

The Facebook team have created a tool, called `TestUtils`, which makes it easy to test React components using any testing framework.

Let's first install it and then we will see what functionalities it provides:

```
npm i --save-dev react-addons-test-utils
```

Now we have everything we need to test our components. The `TestUtils` library has functions to shallow render components or render them into a detached DOM outside the browser. It gives us some utility functions to reference the nodes rendered in the detached DOM so that we can make assertions and expectations on their values.

With TestUtils it is possible to simulate browser events and check whether the event handlers are set up correctly.

Let's start from the beginning by creating a component to test.

The component is a `Button` that will render a button element using the text prop and an event handler for the click event. To start with, we'll create only the skeleton, and we will write the implementation following the tests, using the TDD approach.

We need to implement a class for this component because the TestUtils have some limitations with stateless functional ones.

Let's create a `button.js` file and import `React`:

```
import React from 'react'
```

Now we can define the button as follows:

```
class Button extends React.Component
```

With an empty render function that returns a `div` just to make it work:

```
render() {
  return <div />
}
```

Last but not least we export the button:

```
export default Button
```

The component is now ready to be tested so let's start writing the first test, in a file called `button.spec.js`.

Jest looks into the source folder to find files that end with `.spec`, `.test`, or the ones inside a `__tests__ folder`; but you can change this configuration as you wish to fit the needs of your project.

Inside the `button.spec.js` we first import the dependencies:

```
import React from 'react'
import TestUtils from 'react-addons-test-utils'
import Button from './button'
```

The first one is React, needed to write JSX, the second one is the TestUtils and we will see later how to use it. The last one is the previously created `Button` component.

The very first test that we can write to be sure that everything is working is the following one (I always start in this way):

```
test('works', () => {
  expect(true).toBe(true)
})
```

The `test` function accepts two parameters, with the first one being the description of the test and the second one a function that contains the actual test implementation. There is also a function called `expect` that can be used to make expectations on an object and it can be chained with other functions such as `toBe`, to check if the object passed to expect is the same as the object passed to `toBe`.

If we now open the terminal and run:

```
npm test
```

You should see the following output:

```
PASS   ./button.spec.js
  ✓ works (3ms)
Test Suites: 1 passed, 1 total
Tests:       1 passed, 1 total
Snapshots:   0 total
Time:        1.48s
Ran all test suites.
```

If your console output says PASS you are now ready to write real tests.

As we said, we want to test that the component renders correctly given some props, and that the event handlers do their job.

There are generally two ways of testing React components, by:

- Shallow rendering
- Mounting the components into a detached DOM

The first one is the most simple and easy to understands, we'll start with that. Shallow rendering allows you to render your component *one level deep* and it returns the result of the rendering so that you can run some expectations against it.

Rendering only one level means that we can test our component in isolation and, even if it has some complex children, they do not get rendered and they do not affect the results of the test if they should change or fail.

The first basic test that we can write is checking if the given text is rendered as a child of the button element.

The test starts like this:

```
test('renders with text', () => {
```

As a first operation we define the text variable we pass as a prop and that we will use to check if the right value is rendered:

```
const text = 'text'
```

Now it is time for Shallow rendering, which is implemented in these three lines:

```
const renderer = TestUtils.createRenderer()
renderer.render(<Button text={text} />)
const button = renderer.getRenderOutput()
```

The first one creates the `renderer`, the second one renders the `button` passing the text variable, and finally we get the output of the rendering.

The rendering output is similar to the following object:

```
{ '$$typeof': Symbol(react.element),
    type: 'button',
    key: null,
    ref: null,
    props: { onClick: undefined, children: 'text' },
    _owner: null,
    _store: {} }
```

You may recognize this as a React Element with the `type` property and the props. The second prop is the `children` element, which we want to make sure contains the right value.

Now that we know how the output looks, we can easily write our expectations:

```
expect(button.type).toBe('button')
expect(button.props.children).toBe(text)
```

Here we are declaring that we expect the `button` component to return an element of type `button` with the given text as children.

The last thing to do is to close the test block:

```
})
```

If you now switch to the console and type:

```
npm test
```

You should see something like this:

```
FAIL    ./button.spec.js
  ● renders with text
    expect(received).toBe(expected)
    Expected value to be (using ===):
      "button"
    Received:
      "div"
```

The test fails, and this is something we expect when we run the tests for the first time doing TDD because the component has not been implemented yet. It just returns a `div` element. It's time to go back to the `button` component and make the tests pass. If we change the `render` method to something like:

```
render() {
  return (
    <button>
      {this.props.text}
    </button>
  )
}
```

And we run `npm` test again, we should see a green check mark in our console:

```
PASS   ./button.spec.js
  √ renders with text (9ms)
Test Suites: 1 passed, 1 total
Tests:       1 passed, 1 total
Snapshots:   0 total
Time:        1.629s
Ran all test suites.
```

Congratulations! Your first test on a component written using TDD passed.

Let's now see how we can write a test to check that an `onClick` handler passed to the component gets called when the button is clicked.

Before starting to write the code we should introduce two new concepts: mocks and detached DOM.

The first makes it easy to test the behavior of the functions inside a test. What we want to do here is pass a function to the button using the `onClick` property and verify that the function gets called when the user clicks it.

To do that, we have to create a special function called **mock** (or *spy*, depending on the framework) that behaves like a real function but has some special properties. For example, we can check if it has been called and, if so, how many times and with which parameters.

Jest is an all-in-one testing framework and it gives us all the tools we need to write a proper test. To create a mock function with Jest we can use: `jest.fn()`.

The second thing that we have to learn before writing the next test is that we cannot, using the `TestUtils`, simulate a DOM event using Shallow rendering.

The reason is that, to simulate an event with the `TestUtils`, we need to operate on a real component and not a simple React element.

So, in order to test a browser event, we have to `render` our component into a detached DOM. Rendering a component into a real DOM would require a browser but Jest comes with a special DOM in which we can render our components using the console.

The syntax for rendering a component into the DOM instead of using Shallow rendering is a little bit different; let's see what the test looks like.

We first create a new test block:

```
test('fires the onClick callback', () => {
```

With the title saying that we are going to check for the `onClick` callback to work properly.

Then we create the `onClick` mock, using the `jest` function:

```
const onClick = jest.fn()
```

Here comes the part where we fully render the component into the DOM:

```
const tree = TestUtils.renderIntoDocument(
  <Button onClick={onClick} />
)
```

If we log the tree, we can see that we get back the real component instance and not just the React Element.

For the same reason, we cannot simply inspect the object returned from the `renderIntoDocument` function; instead, we have to use a function from the `TestUtils` library to get the button element that we are looking for:

```
const button = TestUtils.findRenderedDOMComponentWithTag(
  tree,
  'button'
)
```

As the function name suggests, it searches for a component with the given tag name inside the tree.

Now we can use another function from the `TestUtils` to simulate an event:

```
TestUtils.Simulate.click(button)
```

The `Simulate` object accepts a function with the name of the event and the target component as a parameter.

Finally, we write the expectation:

```
expect(onClick).toBeCalled()
```

Here, we have simply said that we expect the `mock` function to be called.

If we run the tests with `npm` test they will fail because the `onClick` functionality hasn't been implemented yet.

```
FAIL   ./button.spec.js
● fires the onClick callback

  expect(jest.fn()).toBeCalled()
  Expected mock function to have been called.
```

This is how the TDD process works. Let's now move back to `button.js` and implement the event handler, modifying the `render` as follows:

```
render() {
  return (
    <button onClick={this.props.onClick}>
      {this.props.text}
    </button>
  )
}
```

If we now run `npm` test again the tests are now green:

```
PASS   ./button.spec.js
  ✓ renders with text (10ms)
  ✓ fires the onClick callback (17ms)
Test Suites: 1 passed, 1 total
Tests:        2 passed, 2 total
Snapshots:    0 total
Time:         1.401s, estimated 2s
Ran all test suites.
```

Our component is fully tested and correctly implemented.

Mocha is a flexible testing framework

In this section, we will see how it's possible to achieve the same results with Mocha in order to make it clear that, with React, you can use any testing framework. Also, it is good to learn the main differences between Jest, which is an integrated test framework and tries to automate all operations to provide a smooth developer experience, and Mocha, which does not make any assumptions on the tools you need. With Mocha, it is up to you to install all the different packages you need to test React in the right way.

Let's create a new folder and initialize a new npm package with:

```
npm init
```

The first thing to install is the mocha package:

```
npm install --save-dev mocha
```

As with Jest, to be able to write ES2015 code and JSX we have to ask Babel for some help: To make it work with Mocha, we have to install the following packages:

```
npm install --save-dev babel-register babel-preset-es2015 babel-preset-react
```

Now that Mocha and Babel have been installed we can set up the test script as follows:

```
"scripts": {
  "test": "mocha --compilers js:babel-register"
},
```

We are telling npm to run mocha as a test task with the compiler flag set in such a way that the JavaScript files are processed using the Babel register.

The next step is installing React and ReactDOM:

```
npm install --save react react-dom
```

And the TestUtils, which we will need to render our components in the test environment:

```
npm install --save-dev react-addons-test-utils
```

The basic functionalities for testing with Mocha are ready but to get feature parity with Jest we need three more packages.

The first one is chai, which lets us write expectations in a similar way to how we wrote them with Jest. The second is chai-spies, which provides the spies functionality that we can use to inspect the onClick callback and check if it has been called.

Last but not least, we must install jsdom, which is the package that we use to create the detached DOM and let the TestUtils do their job in the console without a real browser:

```
npm install --save-dev chai chai-spies jsdom
```

We are now ready to write the tests and we'll use the same `button.js` created earlier. It's already been implemented so we will not follow the TDD process this time, but the goal here is to show the main differences between the two frameworks.

Mocha expects the tests to be in the test folder so we can create it and put a `button.spec.js` file inside it.

The first thing we have to do is import all the dependencies:

```
import chai from 'chai'
import spies from 'chai-spies'
import { jsdom } from 'jsdom'
import React from 'react'
import TestUtils from 'react-addons-test-utils'
import Button from '../button'
```

As you may notice here, there are way more compared to Jest because Mocha gives you the freedom to choose your tools.

The next step is telling `chai` to use the spies package:

```
chai.use(spies)
```

And then we extract the functionalities that we need from the `chai` package. We will use them later in the test implementation:

```
const { expect, spy } = chai
```

Another operation is to set up `jsdom` and provide the DOM object needed to render the React components:

```
global.document = jsdom('')
global.window = document.defaultView
```

Finally, we can write the first test. Typically with Mocha, you have two functions to define your test: the first one is describe, which wraps a set of tests for the same module, and then there is it, which is where tests are implemented.

In this case we describe the behavior of the button:

```
describe('Button', () => {
```

And then we write the first test where we expect the type and the text to be the correct ones:

```
it('renders with text', () => {
```

We define the text variable that we will use to check the validity of the expectation:

```
const text = 'text'
```

We then shallow-render the components as we did before:

```
const renderer = TestUtils.createRenderer()
renderer.render(<Button text={text} />)
const button = renderer.getRenderOutput()
```

And we finally write the expectations:

```
expect(button.type).to.equal('button')
expect(button.props.children).to.equal(text)
```

As you can see, here the syntax is slightly different. Instead of having the `toBe` function, we use the chain `to.equal` provided by `chai`. The result is the same: a comparison between the two values.

Now we can close the first test block:

```
})
```

The second test block where we test that the `onClick callback` is fired looks like this:

```
it('fires the onClick callback', () => {
```

We then create the spy, in a similar way before:

```
const onClick = spy()
```

We render the button into a detached DOM using the `TestUtils`:

```
const tree = TestUtils.renderIntoDocument(
  <Button onClick={onClick} />
)
```

And we use the `tree` to find the component by tag:

```
const button = TestUtils.findRenderedDOMComponentWithTag(
  tree,
  'button'
)
```

The next step is to simulate the button click:

```
TestUtils.Simulate.click(button)
```

Finally, we write the expectation:

```
expect(onClick).to.be.called()
```

Again, the syntax is slightly different but the concept does not change: we check for the spy to be called.

Now, run the `npm` test inside the `root` folder with Mocha, and we should get the following message:

```
Button
  ✓ renders with text
  ✓ fires the onClick callback

2 passing (847ms)
```

This means that our tests have passed and we are now ready to use Mocha to test real components.

JavaScript testing utilities for React

At this point, it should be clear how to test basic components with Jest and Mocha and what the pros and cons are of both.

You have also learned what the TestUtils are and the difference between Shallow rendering and full DOM Rendering.

You may have noticed that the TestUtils, even if they provide a useful tool to help testing components, are verbose and sometimes it is not easy to find the right approach to get the reference to the elements and their properties.

That is the reason why the developers at *AirBnb* decided to create Enzyme, a tool built on top of the TestUtils that makes it easy to manipulate the rendered components.

The API is nicer, similar to jQuery, and it provides many useful utilities to interact with components, their states, and their properties.

Let's see what it means to convert our Jest tests to use Enzyme instead of the TestUtils.

So, please go back to the `Jest` project we previously created and install `enzyme`:

```
npm install --save-dev enzyme
```

Now open the `button.spec.js` and change the import statements to be similar to the following snippets:

```
import React from 'react'
import { shallow } from 'enzyme'
import Button from './button'
```

As you can see, instead of importing the `TestUtils` we are importing the shallow function from Enzyme. As the name suggests the shallow function provides Shallow rendering functionalities and it has some special features.

First of all, with Enzyme it is possible to simulate events even with shallow-rendered elements, which we couldn't do with the `TestUtils`. And, most importantly, the object returned by the function is not a simple React element but rather **ShallowWrapper**, a special object with some useful properties and functions, which we'll look at next.

Let's begin updating the tests, starting with the **renders with text** ones. The first line stays the same because we still need the text variable:

```
const text = 'text'
```

The Shallow rendering part becomes way more simple and intuitive. We can, in fact, replace the three lines of the `TestUtils` with the following one:

```
const button = shallow(<Button text={text} />)
```

The button object represents a ShallowWrapper that has some useful methods that we will use in the new expectation statements:

```
expect(button.type()).toBe('button')
expect(button.text()).toBe(text)
```

As you can see here, instead of checking object properties (they are likely to change as React gets updated), we are using utility functions that abstract the functionalities.

The function `type` returns the type of the rendered elements, and the function `text` returns the text being rendered inside the component. In our case, it's the same text that we passed as prop.

Your test should now look like this:

```
test('renders with text', () => {
  const text = 'text'
  const button = shallow(<Button text={text} />)

  expect(button.type()).toBe('button')
  expect(button.text()).toBe(text)
})
```

This is way more concise and clean than before.

The next thing to do is to update the tests related to the `onClick` event handler. Again, the first line stays the same:

```
const onClick = jest.fn()
```

We still ask Jest to create a mock that we can spy on in the expectations.

We can replace the line where we used the `renderIntoDocument` method to render the component into the detached DOM with the following one:

```
const button = shallow(<Button onClick={onClick} />)
```

We also don't need to find the button with `findRenderedDOMComponentWithTag` because Shallow rendering already references it.

The syntax to simulate an event is slightly different from the `TestUtils` but it is still intuitive:

```
button.simulate('click')
```

Every ShallowWrapper has a `simulate` function that we can call, passing the name of the event and some parameters as a second argument. In this case, we do not need any argument but we will see in the following section how it can be useful when testing forms.

Finally, the expectation remains the same:

```
expect(onClick).toBeCalled()
```

The final code is something like this:

```
test('fires the onClick callback', () => {
  const onClick = jest.fn()
  const button = shallow(<Button onClick={onClick} />)

  button.simulate('click')
```

```
    expect(onClick).toBeCalled()
  })
```

Migrating to Enzyme is relatively easy, and it makes the code more readable.

The library provides some very useful APIs to find nested elements, or to use selectors to search elements given their class names or types.

There are methods to help make assertions and expectations on props, and functions to inject arbitrary state and context into components.

Other than Shallow rendering, which we can use to cover most scenarios, there is a `mount` method that can be imported from the library and renders the tree into the DOM.

A real-world testing example

We have a working test set up and a clear understanding of what the different tools and libraries can do for us. The next thing to do is to test a real-world component.

The `Button` we used in the previous example was great and we should always try to make our components as simple as possible; but sometimes we need to implement different kinds of logic and state, which makes the tests more challenging.

The component we are going to test is **TodoTextInput** from the Redux **TodoMVC** example:

```
https://github.com/reactjs/redux/blob/master/examples/todomvc/src/components
/TodoTextInput.js
```

You can easily copy it into your `Jest` project folder.

It represents a nice example because it has various props, its class names change according to the props it receives, and it has three event handlers that implement a bit of logic that we can test.

The TodoMVC example is a *standard* way of creating a real-world application with the different frameworks in order to compare their features and make it easier for developers to choose.

The result is a simple app that lets users add to-do items and mark them as done. The component we are targeting is the text input used to add and edit items.

It is worth going quickly through the implementation of the component so that we can understand what it does before testing.

First of all, the component is defined using a class:

```
class TodoTextInput extends Component
```

The `propTypes` are defined as a static prop of the class:

```
static propTypes = {
  onSave: PropTypes.func.isRequired,
  text: PropTypes.string,
  placeholder: PropTypes.string,
  editing: PropTypes.bool,
  newTodo: PropTypes.bool
}
```

To make class properties work with Babel we need a plugin called transform-class-properties, which we can easily install with:

```
npm install --save-dev babel-plugin-transform-class-properties
```

And then we add it to the list of Babel plugins in our `.babelrc`:

```
"plugins": ["transform-class-properties"]
```

The state is defined as a `class` property as well:

```
state = {
  text: this.props.text || ''
}
```

Its default value can be the text coming from the props or an empty string.

Then there are three event handlers, which are defined using a `class` property and an arrow function so that they do not need to be manually bound in the constructor.

The first one is the submit handler:

```
handleSubmit = e => {
  const text = e.target.value.trim()
  if (e.which === 13) {
    this.props.onSave(text)
    if (this.props.newTodo) {
      this.setState({ text: '' })
    }
  }
}
```

The function receives the event; it trims the value of the target element, then it checks if the key that fired the event is the *Enter* key (13) and, if it is, it passes the trimmed value to the `onSave` prop function. If the `newTodo` prop is `true`, then the state is set again to an empty string.

The second event handler is the change handler:

```
handleChange = e => {
  this.setState({ text: e.target.value })
}
```

Apart from its being defined as a `class` property you should be able to recognize the method that keeps the state updated for a controlled input element.

The last one is the blur handler:

```
handleBlur = e => {
  if (!this.props.newTodo) {
    this.props.onSave(e.target.value)
  }
}
```

This fires the `onSave` prop function with the value of the field if the prop `newTodo` is `false`.

Finally, there is the `render` method, where the input element is defined with all its properties:

```
render() {
  return (
    <input className={
      classnames({
        edit: this.props.editing,
        'new-todo': this.props.newTodo
      })}
      type="text"
      placeholder={this.props.placeholder}
      autoFocus="true"
      value={this.state.text}
      onBlur={this.handleBlur}
      onChange={this.handleChange}
      onKeyDown={this.handleSubmit} />
  )
}
```

To apply the class name, the `classnames` function is used; it comes from a very useful package, authored by *Jed Watson*, which makes it simple to apply classes using a conditional logic.

Then some static attributes such as `type` and `autofocus` are set, and the value to control the input is set using the `text` property, which is updated on each change. Finally, the event handlers are set to the event properties of the element.

Before starting, it is important to have a clear idea about what we want to test and why. Looking at the component, it is pretty easy to figure out which are the important parts to cover. In this case, it's testing legacy code that we may inherit from other teams, or code that we might find when joining a new company.

The following list represents more or less all the variations and functionalities of the component that are worth testing:

- The state is initialized with the value coming from the props
- The placeholder prop is correctly used in the element
- The right class names are applied following the conditional logic
- The state is updated whenever the value of the field changes
- The onSave callback is fired according to the different states and conditions

It is now time to start writing code and create a file called `TodoTextInput.spec.js` with the following import statements:

```
import React from 'react'
import { shallow } from 'enzyme'
import TodoTextInput from './TodoTextInput'
```

We import React, the Shallow rendering function from Enzyme, and the component to test. We also create a utility function that we will pass to the required `onSave` property in some tests:

```
const noop = () => {}
```

We can now write the first test, where we check that the value passed to the component as a text prop is used as a default value of the element:

```
test('sets the text prop as value', () => {
  const text = 'text'
  const wrapper = shallow(
    <TodoTextInput text={text} onSave={noop} />
  )
```

```
    expect(wrapper.prop('value')).toBe(text)
  })
```

The code is pretty straightforward: We create a text variable, which we pass to the component when we shallow-render it. As you can see, we pass the `noop` utility function to the `onSave` prop because we do not care about it, but it is required and React would complain if we passed `null`.

Finally, we render the component and check that the value prop of the output element is equal to the given text. If we now run `npm` test in the console we can see the following output, which means that the test passes:

```
PASS   ./TodoTextInput.spec.js
  ✓ sets the text prop as value (10ms)
Test Suites: 1 passed, 1 total
Tests:       1 passed, 1 total
Snapshots:   0 total
Time:        1.384s
Ran all test suites.
```

Awesome, let's continue with the next tests. The second test is pretty similar to the first one, except that we test the `placeholder` property:

```
test('uses the placeholder prop', () => {
  const placeholder = 'placeholder'
  const wrapper = shallow(
    <TodoTextInput placeholder={placeholder} onSave={noop} />
  )

  expect(wrapper.prop('placeholder')).toBe(placeholder)
})
```

If we run `npm` test, it will now tell us that the two tests are green.

Let's now delve into some more interesting stuff and test whether the class names get applied to the element when the related props are present:

```
test('applies the right class names', () => {
  const wrapper = shallow(
    <TodoTextInput editing newTodo onSave={noop} />
  )

  expect(wrapper.hasClass('edit new-todo')).toBe(true)
})
```

In this test we add the editing and `newTodo` props and we check inside the expect function that the classes have been applied to the output.

We could check the classes separately to make sure that one is not affecting the other but you should get the point.

Now the tests start getting more complex because we want to test the behavior of the component when the key down event happens.

In particular, we want to check that, if the *Enter* key is pressed, the `onSave` callback gets called with the value of the element:

```
test('fires onSave on enter', () => {
  const onSave = jest.fn()
  const value = 'value'
  const wrapper = shallow(<TodoTextInput onSave={onSave} />)

  wrapper.simulate('keydown', { target: { value }, which: 13 })

  expect(onSave).toHaveBeenCalledWith(value)
})
```

We first create a mock using the `jest.fn()` function; we then create a value variable to store the value of the event, which we also use to double-check that the function gets called with the same value. Then we'll render the component and finally we'll simulate the key down event passing an event object.

The event object has two properties: the target, which represents the element that initiated the event and has a `value` property, which represents the key code of the key that has been pressed.

The expectation here is that the mock `onSave` callback gets called with the value of the event.

The npm test now tells us that four tests have passed.

A similar test to the previous one can check that, if the pressed key is not the *Enter* key, nothing happens:

```
test('does not fire onSave on key down', () => {
  const onSave = jest.fn()
  const wrapper = shallow(<TodoTextInput onSave={onSave} />)

  wrapper.simulate('keydown', { target: { value: '' } })

  expect(onSave).not.toBeCalled()
})
```

The test is pretty similar to the previous one but it is important to notice the difference in the expect statement. We are using a new property, `.not`, which asserts the opposite on the following function; in this case `toBeCalled` is supposed to be `false`.

As you can see, the way we write expectations is very similar to the spoken language.

With five green tests, we can move into the next one:

```
test('clears the value after save if new', () => {
  const value = 'value'
  const wrapper = shallow(<TodoTextInput newTodo onSave={noop} />)

  wrapper.simulate('keydown', { target: { value }, which: 13 })

  expect(wrapper.prop('value')).toBe('')
})
```

The difference with the previous test is that now there is the `newTodo` prop on the element, which forces the value to be reset.

Running `npm` test in the console gives us a green bar with six passed tests.

The following test is a very common one:

```
test('updates the text on change', () => {
  const value = 'value'
  const wrapper = shallow(<TodoTextInput onSave={noop} />)

  wrapper.simulate('change', { target: { value } })

  expect(wrapper.prop('value')).toBe(value)
})
```

This test checks that the controlled input works properly and, if you think about the forms we discussed in Chapter 6, *Write Code for the Browser*, this is a must-have for all the forms in your application.

We simulate the change event passing a set value and we check that the `value` property of the output element is equal to it.

The green tests are now seven in total and there is only one more to go.

In the last test we check that the blur event fires the callback only when the To-do item is not new:

```
test('fires onSave on blur if not new', () => {
  const onSave = jest.fn()
  const value = 'value'
  const wrapper = shallow(<TodoTextInput onSave={onSave} />)

  wrapper.simulate('blur', { target: { value } })

  expect(onSave).toHaveBeenCalledWith(value)
})
```

We set up a mock, create the expected value, simulate the blur event using the target, and then we check that the onSave callback has been called with the given value.

If we run npm test now, everything should be green and the list of passed tests is now pretty long:

```
PASS   ./TodoTextInput.spec.js
  ✓ sets the text prop as value (10ms)
  ✓ uses the placeholder prop (1ms)
  ✓ applies the right class names (1ms)
  ✓ fires onSave on enter (3ms)
  ✓ does not fire onSave on key down (1ms)
  ✓ clears the value after save if new (5ms)
  ✓ updates the text on change (1ms)
  ✓ fires onSave on blur if not new (2ms)
Test Suites: 1 passed, 1 total
Tests:       8 passed, 8 total
Snapshots:   0 total
Time:        2.271s
Ran all test suites.
```

Good job, the component is now covered with tests; and if we need to refactor it, change its behavior, or add some features, the tests will help us to discover whether the new code breaks any of the old functionalities.

This makes us more confident with our code so that we can touch any line without worrying about regressions.

React tree Snapshot Testing

Now that you have seen a real-world testing example you may think that writing so many tests for a single component is a time-consuming task and not worth it.

Checking for each variation of text, value, and class name is laborious and it requires much code to cover all instances. However, most of the time, whenever we test components, the most important thing for us is that the output is correct and that it does not change unexpectedly. There is a new feature introduced in Jest that helps with this problem and it's called **Snapshot Testing**.

Snapshots are *pictures* of the component with some props at a given point in time. Every time we run the tests, Jest creates new *pictures* and it compares them with the previous ones to check if something has changed.

The content of the snapshot is the output of the `render` method of a package called `react-test-renderer`, which has to be installed with the following command:

```
npm install --save-dev react-test-renderer
```

Once the test rendered is ready, we can create a new file called `TodoTextInput-snapshot.spec.js` with the following import statements:

```
import React from 'react'
import renderer from 'react-test-renderer'
import TodoTextInput from './TodoTextInput'
```

We import React to be able to use JSX, the `renderer` that creates the tree for the snapshot, and finally the target component that we want to test.

All the dependencies are now available and we can write a simple test:

```
test('snapshots are awesome', () => {
```

In the first line we render the component using the `renderer` that we previously imported:

```
const component = renderer.create(
  <TodoTextInput onSave={() => {}} />
)
```

What we receive back is the instance of the component, which has a special function called `toJSON` that we call in the following line:

```
const tree = component.toJSON()
```

The resulting tree is the React element returned from the original component that Jest will use to generate the snapshot to be compared with the next ones.

If we log the tree in the console, we can see what it looks like:

```
{ type: 'input',
      props:
        { className: '',
          type: 'text',
          placeholder: undefined,
          autoFocus: 'true',
          value: '',
          onBlur: [Function],
          onChange: [Function],
          onKeyDown: [Function] },
      children: null }
```

Finally, we write the expectation statement checking if the tree matches the previously saved snapshot:

```
expect(tree).toMatchSnapshot()
```

The first time we run the tests with npm test the snapshot is newly created and stored in a `__snapshots__` folder.

Each file inside that folder represents a snapshot. If we look into it we don't find the React element object, but a human-readable version of the rendered output:

```
exports[`test snapshots are awesome 1`] = `
<input
  autoFocus="true"
  className=""
  onBlur={[Function]}
  onChange={[Function]}
  onKeyDown={[Function]}
  placeholder={undefined}
  type="text"
  value="" />
`;
```

If we now go back to the test, add the `editing` prop to the component, and run `npm` test again, we get the following response in the console:

```
FAIL   ./TodoTextInput-snapshot.spec.js
 ● snapshots are awesome
   expect(value).toMatchSnapshot()
   Received value does not match stored snapshot 1.
   - Snapshot
   + Received
   @@ -1,8 +1,8 @@
    <input
      autoFocus="true"
   -   className=""
   +   className="edit"
      onBlur={[Function]}
      onChange={[Function]}
      onKeyDown={[Function]}
      placeholder={undefined}
      type="text"
```

It shows us what's changed in the current snapshot. In this case, it's the `className` property, which was empty before and now contains the edit string.

A few lines below, we can see this message:

```
Inspect your code changes or run with npm test -- -u to update
them.
```

Snapshots make the developer experience incredibly smooth; with a simple flag, we can confirm if the new Snapshot reflects the correct version of the component. Running `npm` test `-- -u` updates the snapshot automatically.

If the component has been changed by mistake instead, we can go back to the code and fix it.

As you can see, Snapshot Testing is a powerful feature that makes testing components easier and helps developers save time by avoiding the need to write tests for all the variants.

Code coverage tools

There are many reasons to write tests and we went through some of them in the previous section. The main one is always to provide value to our codebase and make it more robust.

Because of that, I am always skeptical when it comes to counting the number of tests, the lines of code, and the test coverage. I suggest people don't focus on numbers but on the value that the tests can provide.

However, in some scenarios it is useful to get some measurement of the coverage and keep track of the numbers. In big projects with many different modules, doing so makes it easy to spot files that have not been adequately tested or that have not been tested at all.

Once again, Jest provides all the equipment you need to run your tests and of course it provides the functionalities to measure and store the code coverage information.

It uses Istanbul, one of the most popular code coverage libraries, which you will have to install manually if you are using Mocha.

Running the coverage with Jest is pretty straightforward: You just need to add the -- coverage flag to the `Jest` command in the `npm` scripts. Alternatively, you can create a configuration section for Jest in `package.json` and set the `collectCoverage` option to true.

```
"jest": {
  "collectCoverage": true
}
```

If you now run `npm` test again you can see a different output in the console, where a table shows some information about the coverage:

File	% Stmts	% Branch	% Funcs	% Lines	Uncovered Lines
All files	100	87.5	100	100	
TodoTextInput.js	100	87.5	100	100	

As you can see, our file is almost fully covered. The first column shows how many statements are covered; the second column shows the different branches of conditional statements; the third measures the functions that have been tested; and the fourth column shows the lines of code covered by tests. The last column, which is currently empty, would tell you which lines are uncovered, and that is pretty useful information when it comes to quickly finding the parts of the code that need more attention.

Currently, the only value that is not 100% covered is the branches and, in fact, I left one branch of the last test uncovered on purpose so we can achieve full coverage together.

If you open the `TodoTextInput.js` file and check the `onBlur` handler, you'll notice that there are two branches:

```
handleBlur = e => {
  if (!this.props.newTodo) {
    this.props.onSave(e.target.value)
  }
}
```

When the to-do is not new, the `onSave` prop function is fired with the current value of the field; when the to-do is new nothing happens.

We have tested only the first path, which is the most obvious but often it's worth testing all the different branches to make sure that everything is working properly.

Let's move back to the `TodoTextInput.spec.js` and add a new test:

```
test('does not fire onSave on blur if new', () => {
  const onSave = jest.fn()
  const wrapper = shallow(
    <TodoTextInput newTodo onSave={onSave} />
  )

  wrapper.simulate('blur')

  expect(onSave).not.toBeCalled()
})
```

The test is similar to the last one in the file except that we pass the `newTodo` prop to the component and we check that the `onSave` callback does not get called.

If we now run npm test again, we can see that all the columns are now showing 100%.

Common testing solutions

In this last section about testing, we will go through some common patterns that are useful to know when testing complex components.

Testing components should now be familiar to you, and you should have all the information to start writing tests for your applications. However, sometimes is not easy to figure out the best strategy to test, for example, **Higher-Order Components**.

Testing Higher-Order Components

As we have seen in previous chapters, we can use Higher-Order Components to share functionalities between different components across the application. HoCs are functions that take a component and return an enhanced version of it.

Testing this kind of component is not as intuitive as testing simple ones, so it is worth looking at some common solutions together.

Our target component is going to be the withData HoC created in Chapter 5, *Proper Data Fetching*. We will only apply a small variation in the way data fetching is performed.

The withData function has the following signature:

```
const withData = URL => Component => (...)
```

It takes the URL of the endpoint where the data has to be loaded, and it provides such data to the target component. The URL can be a function that receives the current props or a static string.

The withData function returns a class defined as follows:

```
class extends React.Component
```

With a constructor where the data is initialized:

```
constructor(props) {
  super(props)

  this.state = { data: [] }
}
```

The data is loaded in the componentDidMount lifecycle hook:

```
componentDidMount() {
  const endpoint = typeof url === 'function'
    ? url(this.props)
    : url

  getJSON(endpoint).then(data => this.setState({ data }))
}
```

As you can see, there is a small difference from the example in Chapter 5, *Proper Data Fetching*, because, instead of using the fetch function directly, we are using getJSON so that you can learn how to mock external modules.

It is also best practice to wrap third-party libraries and abstract API calls into separate modules, so when we test a component we can isolate it from its dependencies.

The `getJSON` function is imported at the top of the file:

```
import getJSON from './get-json'
```

It returns a promise with the JSON data retrieved from the endpoint.

Finally, we `render` the target component spreading the props and the state:

```
render() {
  return <Component {...this.props} {...this.state} />
}
```

Now, there are a few different things that we want to cover with tests in this function and we will start with the most simple ones. For example, a simple task could be to check whether the props received from the enhanced component are correctly passed to the target.

After that, we'd test if the logic of creating the endpoint from the URL works for both function and static strings.

Ultimately, we want to test that, as soon as the `getJSON` function returns the data, the target component receives it.

In the test file we first load all the dependencies:

```
import React from 'react'
import { shallow, mount } from 'enzyme'
import withData from './with-data'
import getJSON from './get-json'
```

We are importing both the `shallow` and `mount` functions from Enzyme because the simple tests can be run without the DOM, but since we need to test what happens during the lifecycle hooks we need `mount` as well.

Then, we create a couple of variables that we will use within the tests:

```
const data = 'data'
const List = () => <div />
```

This is the mock data that we use to check whether the information is correctly passed from the fetch to the component, and a dummy `List` component.

Creating a dummy component is pretty common practice when testing HoC because we need a target component to enhance, so we can figure out if all the features are correctly working.

Now comes the hardest part and the most powerful one:

```
jest.mock('./get-json', () => (
  jest.fn(() => ({ then: callback => callback(data) }))
))
```

As we said, we are using an external component to fetch the data. One thing that we want to avoid is loading real data and, most importantly, we do not want our test to fail if the external module fails for some reasons. With Jest it is very easy to isolate and mock the dependencies.

Using the `jest.mock` function we are telling the test runner to replace the external module with the function we passed as a second parameter. The function returns a mock function from `jest.fn` returns an object that looks like a promise but is synchronous. It has a then function that fires the received callback, passing to it the fake data we previously defined.

From now on we can unit-test the Higher-Order Component without worrying about the behavior or the bugs of the `getJSON` function.

We are now ready to write the real tests, with the first one being where we check if the props are passed correctly down to the target:

```
test('passes the props to the component', () => {
  const ListWithGists = withData()(List)
  const username = 'gaearon'

  const wrapper = shallow(<ListWithGists username={username} />)

  expect(wrapper.prop('username')).toBe(username)
})
```

It should be pretty clear, but let's see together what it does. We first enhance the dummy `List` that we are passing to the HoC, we then define a prop that we pass to the component and we shallow-render it.

Finally, we check if the output has a prop with the same value. Great; if we run npm test we see that the first test passes.

Let's now move to the tests that require mounting the component to the detached DOM. First of all, we check whether both the URL function and the static string work. The static string is pretty easy to test:

```
test('uses the string url', () => {
  const url = 'https://api.github.com/users/gaearon/gists'
  const withGists = withData(url)
  const ListWithGists = withGists(List)

  mount(<ListWithGists />)

  expect(getJSON).toHaveBeenCalledWith(url)
})
```

We define a URL and we use the partial application to generate a new function; we then use it to enhance the dummy `List`.

Then, we mount the component and check that the `getJSON` function is called with the URL that we passed. Easy: two green tests.

Now we want to check if the URL function works:

```
test('uses the function url', () => {
  const url = jest.fn(props => (
    `https://api.github.com/users/${props.username}/gists`
  )
  const withGists = withData(url)
  const ListWithGists = withGists(List)
  const props = { username: 'gaearon' }

  mount(<ListWithGists {...props} />)

  expect(url).toHaveBeenCalledWith(props)
  expect(getJSON).toHaveBeenCalledWith(
    'https://api.github.com/users/gaearon/gists'
  )
})
```

We first generate the URL function using a Jest mock so that we can write an expectation on it, then we enhance the `List` and define the prop that gets passed to the component.

Finally, we write two expectations:

- The first one checks that the URL function has been called with the given props
- The second one checks again that the `getJSON` function is fired with the right endpoint

Now comes the final part where we check that the data returned to the `getJSON` module is passed correctly to the target component:

```
test('passes the data to the component', () => {
  const ListWithGists = withData()(List)

  const wrapper = mount(<ListWithGists />)

  expect(wrapper.prop('data')).toEqual(data)
})
```

We first enhance the `List` using the HoC, we then mount the component, and we save a reference of the wrapper. Then we search for the `List` component inside the mounted wrapper and check that its `data` property is the same as the data returned from the fetching.

If we run `npm` test again we see that four tests are now passing.

What you learned in this section is how to test Higher-Order Components using a dummy child and how to isolate the current component mocking external dependencies.

The Page Object pattern

Let's now move into another common way of writing tests when the tree of components becomes more complex and there are multiple nested children.

For this example, we will use the **Controlled form component** created in `Chapter 6`, *Write Code for the Browser*:

```
class Controlled extends React.Component
```

Let's go quickly through its function to remind ourselves how it works, and then we can talk about testing.

Inside the `constructor` we initialize the state and bind the handlers:

```
constructor(props) {
  super(props)

  this.state = {
    firstName: 'Dan',
    lastName: 'Abramov',
  }

  this.handleChange = this.handleChange.bind(this)
```

```
    this.handleSubmit = this.handleSubmit.bind(this)
  }
```

The `handleChange` handler keeps the value of the fields updated inside the state:

```
handleChange({ target }) {
  this.setState({
    [target.name]: target.value,
  })
}
```

Then there is the `handleSubmit` handler, where we use the `preventDefault` function of the event object to disable the default behavior of the browser when the form is submitted. We also call the `onSubmit` prop function received from the parent, passing it the value of the fields concatenated.

This last function was not present in the original controlled example, but we need it here it to show how to test the component properly:

```
handleSubmit(e) {
  e.preventDefault()

  this.props.onSubmit(
    `${this.state.firstName} ${this.state.lastName}`
  )
}
```

Last but not least, we have the `render` method where we define the fields and we attach the handler functions:

```
render() {
  return (
    <form onSubmit={this.handleSubmit}>
      <input
        type="text"
        name="firstName"
        value={this.state.firstName}
        onChange={this.handleChange}
      />
      <input
        type="text"
        name="lastName"
        value={this.state.lastName}
        onChange={this.handleChange}
      />
      <button>Submit</button>
    </form>
```

```
   )
}
```

One basic functionality that we may want to test here is typing something into the fields and submitting the form results in the `onSumbit` callback being called with the entered values.

It should be clear to you how to write a simple test to cover this case with Enzyme, so let's check it together:

```
test('submits the form', () => {
```

First of all we define an `onSubmit` mock function using Jest and we mount the component storing a reference to the wrapper:

```
const onSubmit = jest.fn()
const wrapper = shallow(<Controlled onSubmit={onSubmit} />)
```

Secondly, we find the first field and we fire the change event on it, passing the value that we want to update:

```
const firstName = wrapper.find('[name="firstName"]')
firstName.simulate(
  'change',
  { target: { name: 'firstName', value: 'Christopher' } }
)
```

We then do the same thing with the second field:

```
const lastName = wrapper.find('[name="lastName"]')
lastName.simulate(
  'change',
  { target: { name: 'lastName', value: 'Chedeau' } }
)
```

Once the fields are updated, we submit the form simulating an event:

```
const form = wrapper.find('form')
form.simulate('submit', { preventDefault: () => {} })
```

Now, let's write the expectations:

```
expect(onSubmit).toHaveBeenCalledWith('Christopher Chedeau')
```

And close the test block:

```
})
```

Running npm test in the console shows a green message, which is good; but if you look at the implementation of the test you can easily spot some problems and potential optimization issues.

The most visible one is that the code for filling the fields is duplicated, apart from some variables. The code is verbose and, most importantly, it's coupled with the structure of the markup.

If we have multiple tests like this and then we change the markup, we have to update the code in many parts of the file. Wouldn't it be nice to remove the duplication and move the selectors to one single place so that it is easier to change them if the form changes?

This is where the **Page Object pattern** come to the rescue. If we create a Page object that represents the elements of the page and hides the selectors, and we use it to fill the fields and submit the form, we'll get many benefits and avoid duplicated code.

It is fair to say that usually being **Don't Repeat Yourself (DRY)** in the tests is not the best approach because the risk is to add more bugs and complexity, but in this case it is worth it.

Let's see how the controlled form test can be improved thanks to the Page Object pattern.

First of all we have to create a Page object using a class:

```
class Page
```

The class has a constructor that receives the root wrapper from Enzyme and stores it for future usage:

```
constructor(wrapper) {
  this.wrapper = wrapper
}
```

Then we define a generic function to fill the fields that accepts name and values and fires the change event:

```
fill(name, value) {
  const field = this.wrapper.find(`[name="${name}"]`)
  field.simulate('change', { target: { name, value } })
}
```

Then we implement a `submit` function to abstract the part where we look for the button and simulate the browser event:

```
submit() {
  const form = this.wrapper.find('form')
  form.simulate('submit', { preventDefault() {} })
}
```

We are now able to rewrite the previous test in the following way:

```
test('submits the form with the page object', () => {
  const onSubmit = jest.fn()
  const wrapper = shallow(<Controlled onSubmit={onSubmit} />)

  const page = new Page(wrapper)
  page.fill('firstName', 'Christopher')
  page.fill('lastName', 'Chedeau')
  page.submit()

  expect(onSubmit).toHaveBeenCalledWith('Christopher Chedeau')
})
```

As you can see, we created an instance of the Page Object and we used its function to fill the fields and submit the form.

With the Page Object the code looks much cleaner and has no unnecessary repetitions. If something changes in the component, instead of updating multiple tests, we can just modify the way the Page Object works in a transparent and easy way.

React Dev Tools

When testing in the console is not enough, and we want to inspect our application while it is running inside the browser, we can use the React Developer Tools.

You can install them as a Chrome extension from the following URL:

```
https://chrome.google.com/webstore/detail/react-developer-tools/fmkadmapgofa
dopljbjfkapdkoienihi?hl=en
```

The installation adds a tab to the Chrome Dev Tools called **React** where you can inspect the rendered tree of components and check which properties they have received and what their state is at a particular point in time.

Props and state can be read, and they can be changed in real time to trigger updates in the UI and see the results straightaway.

This is a must-have tool and in the most recent versions it has a new feature that can be enabled by ticking the **Trace React Updates** checkbox.

When this functionality is enabled we can use our application and visually see which components get updated when we perform a particular action. The updated components are highlighted with colored rectangles and it becomes easy to spot possible optimizations.

Error handling with React

Even if we write excellent code and we cover all the code with tests, errors will still happen. The different browsers and environments, and real user data, are all variables that we cannot control and sometimes our code will fail. As developers, that is something we must accept.

The best thing we can do when problems happen in our applications is:

- Notify the users and help them understand what happened and what they should do
- Collect all useful information about the error and the state of the application in order to reproduce it and fix bugs quickly

The way React handle errors is slightly counter-intuitive in the beginning.

Suppose you have the following components:

```
const Nice => <div>Nice</div>
```

And:

```
const Evil => (
  <div>
    Evil
    {this.does.not.exist}
  </div>
)
```

Rendering the following `App` into the DOM, we would expect different things to happen:

```
const App = () => (
  <div>
    <Nice />
    <Evil />
    <Nice />
  </div>
)
```

We may expect, for example, that the first `Nice` component gets rendered and the rendering stops because `Evil` throws an exception. Otherwise, we might expect both `Nice` components to be rendered and the `Evil` not to be shown. What really happens is that nothing is displayed on the screen.

In React, if one single component throws an exception, it stops rendering the entire tree. This is a decision made to improve safety and avoid inconsistent states.

Wouldn't it be nice if the broken component fail, in isolation, letting the rest of the tree keep on rendering? The only possible way to achieve this result would be by monkey-patching the render method and wrapping it into a `try...catch` block. That's clearly bad practice and it should be avoided; but in some cases it can be useful for debugging.

There is a library called `react-component-errors` monkey-patches all the component's methods and wraps them into a `try...catch` block so that they do not make the entire tree fail.

This approach has a downside in terms of performance and compatibility with the library, but as soon as you understand the risks you can choose to try it.

We first install the library using:

```
npm install --save react-component-errors
```

Then we import it inside your component file:

```
import wrapReactLifecycleMethods from 'react-component-errors'
```

And then we decorate your classes in the following way:

```
@wrapReactLifecycleMethods
class MyComponents extends React.Component
```

This library not only avoids breaking the entire tree when a single components fails, but it also provides a way to set a custom error handler and get some valuable information when an exception occurs.

We have to import the `config` object from the package like this:

```
import { config } from 'react-component-errors'
```

Then, we can set a custom error handler in the following way:

```
config.errorHandler = errorReport => { ... }
```

The function that we define as `errorHandler` receives an error report containing useful information to reproduce and fix the error.

The report, in fact, apart from the original error object, gives us the component name and the function name that generated the issue. It also provides all the props that the component received. All this information should be enough to write a test, reproduce the issue, and fix it quickly.

It is worth stressing that the technique used by this library should be avoided, and it could create some problems with your application. Most importantly, it should be disabled in production.

Summary

In this chapter, you learned about the benefits of testing, and the frameworks you can use to cover your React components with tests. Jest is a *fully-featured tool* while Mocha lets you *customize your experience*.

The TestUtils let you *render your components* outside a browser and Enzyme is a powerful tool to *access the output of rendering* within the tests. We have seen how to test components using mocks and writing expectations.

We learned how Snapshot Testing can make it even easier to test the output of components and its code coverage tools helps you monitor the testing state of the codebase.

It is important to bear in mind common solutions when it comes to testing complex components such as Higher-Order Cmponents or forms with multiples nested fields.

Finally, you have learned how the React Developer Tools help debugging and how to approach error handling in React.

11
Anti-Patterns to Be Avoided

With this book, you've learned how to apply best practices when writing a React application. In the first chapters we revisited the basic concepts to build a solid understanding, and then we took a leap into more advanced techniques in the following chapters.

You now should be able to build reusable components, make components communicate with each other, and optimize an application tree to get the best performance. However, developers make mistakes, and this chapter is all about the common anti-patterns we should avoid when using React.

Looking at common errors will help you to avoid them and will aid your understanding of how React works and how to build applications in the React way. For each problem, we will see an example that shows how to reproduce and solve it.

In this chapter we will cover the following points:

- The scenarios where initializing the state using props leads to unexpected results
- Why mutating the state is wrong and harmful for performance
- How to choose the right keys and help the reconciler
- Why spreading props on DOM elements is bad and what you should be doing instead

Initializing the state using props

In this section, we will see how initializing the state using props received from the parent is usually an anti-pattern. I have used the word *usually* because, as we will see, once we have it clear in our mind what the problems with this approach are, we might still decide to use it.

One of the best ways to learn something is by looking at the code, so we will start by creating a simple component with a + button to increment a counter.

The component is implemented using a `class`:

```
class Counter extends React.Component
```

It has a `constructor` where we initialize the state using the `count` prop and we bind the event handler:

```
constructor(props) {
  super(props)

  this.state = {
    count: props.count,
  }

  this.handleClick = this.handleClick.bind(this)
}
```

The implementation of the click handler is pretty straightforward: we just add 1 to the current count value and store the resulting value back into the state:

```
handleClick() {
  this.setState({
    count: this.state.count + 1,
  })
}
```

Finally, in the `render` method, we describe the output, which is composed by the current value of the count, and the button to increment it:

```
render() {
  return (
    <div>
      {this.state.count}
      <button onClick={this.handleClick}>+</button>
    </div>
  )
}
```

Now let's render this component, passing 1 as the `count` prop:

```
<Counter count={1} />
```

It works as expected: each click on the + button increments the current value. So, what's the problem?

There are two main errors:

- We have a duplicated source of truth
- If the count prop passed to the component changes, the state does not get updated

If we inspect the `Counter` element using the React Developer Tools, we notice that `Props` and `State` hold a similar value:

```
<Counter>
Props
   count: 1
State
   count: 1
```

This makes it unclear which is the current and trustworthy value to use inside the component and to display to the user.

Even worse, clicking + once makes the values diverge:

```
<Counter>
Props
   count: 1
State
   count: 2
```

At this point, we can assume that the second value represents the current count but this is not explicit and can lead to unexpected behaviors or wrong values down in the tree.

The second problem centers on how the class is created and instantiated by React. The constructor function of the class gets called only once when the component is created.

In our `Counter` component we read the value of the `count` prop and we stored it into the state. If the value of that prop changes during the lifecycle of the application (let's say, it becomes `10`), the `Counter` component will never use the new value, because it has already been initialized. This puts the component into an inconsistent state, which is not optimal and hard to debug.

What if we really want to use the prop's value to initialize the component and we know for sure that the value does not change in the future?

In that case, it's best practice to make it explicit and give the prop a name that makes your intentions clear, such as `initialCount`. For example, if we change the `constructor` of the `Counter` component in the following way:

```
constructor(props) {
  super(props)

  this.state = {
    count: props.initialCount,
  }

  this.handleClick = this.handleClick.bind(this)
}
```

And then we use it like this:

```
<Counter initialCount={1} />
```

It is clear that the parent only has a way to initialize the counter but any future values of the `initialCount` prop will be ignored.

Mutating the state

React comes with a very clear and straightforward API to mutate the internal state of components. Using the `setState` function, we can tell the library how we want the state to be changed. As soon as the state is updated, React re-renders the component and we can access the new state through the `this.state` property. That's it.

Sometimes, however, we could make the mistake of mutating the state object directly, leading to dangerous consequences for the component's consistency and performance.

First of all, if we mutate the state without using `setState`, two bad things can happen:

- The state changes without making the component re-render
- Whenever `setState` gets called in future, the mutated state gets applied

If we go back to the counter example and change the click handler to:

```
handleClick() {
  this.state.count++
}
```

We can see how clicking + does not affect the rendered value in the browser but, if we look into the component using the React Developer Tools, the value of the state is correctly updated. This is an inconsistent state and we surely do not want it in our applications.

If you are doing it by mistake, you can easily fix it by using the setState API; but if you find yourself doing it on purpose, for example to avoid the component re-rendering, you had better re-think the structure of your components.

As we have seen in Chapter 3, *Create Truly Reusable Components*, in fact, one of the reasons why we use the state object is to store values that are needed inside the render method.

The second problem that occurs when the state is mutated directly is that, whenever setState is called in any other part of the component, the mutated state gets applied unexpectedly.

For example, if we keep on working on the Counter component and we add the following button, which updates the state creating a new foo property:

```
<button onClick={() => this.setState({ foo: 'bar' })}>
  Update
</button>
```

We can see how clicking the + does not have any visible effect but as soon as we click Update the count value in the browser makes a jump, displaying the current hidden state count value.

This uncontrolled behavior is something we want to avoid as well.

Last but not least, mutating the state has a severe impact on performance. To show this behavior, we are going to create a new component, similar to the list we used in Chapter 9, *Improve the Performance of Your Applications*, when we learned how to use keys and PureComponent.

Changing the value of the state has a negative impact when using PureComponent. To understand the problem we are going to create the following List:

```
class List extends React.PureComponent
```

Inside its constructor we initialize the list with two items and bind the event handler:

```
constructor(props) {
  super(props)

  this.state = {
    items: ['foo', 'bar'],
```

```
    }

    this.handleClick = this.handleClick.bind(this)
  }
```

The click handler is pretty simple: it just pushes a new element into the array (we will see later why that is wrong) and then it sets the array back into the state:

```
handleClick() {
  this.state.items.push('baz')

  this.setState({
    items: this.state.items,
  })
}
```

Finally, we use the render method to display the current length of the list and the button that triggers the handler:

```
render() {
  return (
    <div>
      {this.state.items.length}
      <button onClick={this.handleClick}>+</button>
    </div>
  )
}
```

Looking at the code, we might think that there are no issues; but, if we run the component inside the browser, we'll notice that the value doesn't get updated when we click **+**.

Even in this case, by checking the state of the component using the React Developer Tool we can see how the state has been updated internally, without causing a re-render:

```
<List>
State
  items: Array[3]
    0: "foo"
    1: "bar"
    2: "baz"
```

The reason why we experience the inconsistency is because we mutated the array instead of providing a new value.

Pushing a new item into the array, in fact, does not create a new array. The `PureComponent` decides if the component should be updated by checking if the values of its props and state are changed but, in this case, we passed the same array again. This can be counter-intuitive in the beginning, especially if you are not used to working with immutable data structures.

The point here is always to set a new value of the `state` property and we can easily fix the issue by changing the click handler of the `List` component in the following way:

```
handleClick() {
  this.setState({
    items: this.state.items.concat('baz'),
  })
}
```

The `concat` function of the array returns a new array appending the new item to the previous ones. In this way, `PureComponent` finds a new array in the state and re-renders itself correctly.

Using indexes as a key

In Chapter 9, *Improve the Performance of Your Applications*, talking about performance and the reconciler, we have seen how we can help React figure out the shortest path to update the DOM by using the `key` prop.

The key prop uniquely identifies an element in the DOM and React uses it to check if the element is new or if it has to be updated when the component props or state change.

Using keys is always a good idea and, if you don't do it, React gives a warning in the console (in development mode). However, it is not simply a matter of using a key; sometimes the value that we decide to use as a key can make the difference. In fact, using the wrong key can give us unexpected behaviors in some instances. In this section, we will see one of those instances.

Let's, again, create a `List` component:

```
class List extends React.PureComponent
```

In the constructor, the items are initialized and the handlers bound to the component:

```
constructor(props) {
  super(props)

  this.state = {
    items: ['foo', 'bar'],
```

```
    }

    this.handleClick = this.handleClick.bind(this)
  }
```

The implementation of the click handler is slightly different from the previous one because in this case we need to insert a new item at the top of the list:

```
handleClick() {
  const items = this.state.items.slice()
  items.unshift('baz')

  this.setState({
    items,
  })
}
```

Finally, in the `render` method we show the list and the + button to add the **baz** item at the top of the list:

```
render() {
  return (
    <div>
      <ul>
        {this.state.items.map((item, index) => (
          <li key={index}>{item}</li>
        ))}
      </ul>
      <button onClick={this.handleClick}>+</button>
    </div>
  )
}
```

If you run the component inside the browser you will not see any problems: clicking the + button inserts a new item at the top of the list. But let's do an experiment.

We change the `render` method in the following way, adding an input field near each item. We use an input field because we can edit its content, making it easier to figure out the problem:

```
render() {
  return (
    <div>
      <ul>
        {this.state.items.map((item, index) => (
          <li key={index}>
            {item}
            <input type="text" />
```

```
          </li>
        ))}
      </ul>
      <button onClick={this.handleClick}>+</button>
    </div>
  )
}
```

If we run this component again in the browser, copy the values of the items in the input fields, and then click +, we will get an unexpected behavior.

As shown in the following screenshot, the items shift down while the input elements remain in the same position in such a way that their value does not match the value of the items anymore:

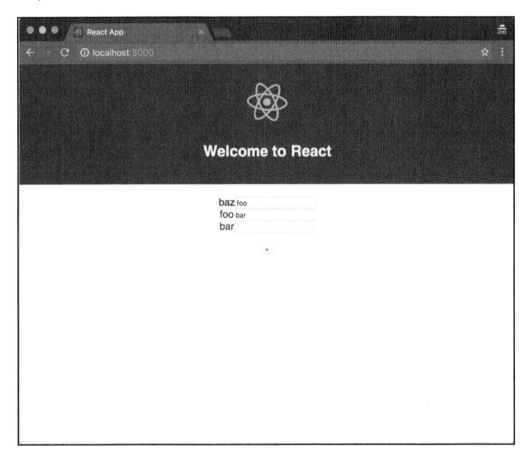

To investigate and figure out the cause of the problem, we can install the **Perf Add-on** and import it inside the component:

```
import Perf from 'react-addons-perf'
```

We can then use two lifecycle hooks to store the information about the way React manipulates the DOM and print them in the console:

```
componentWillUpdate() {
  Perf.start()
}

componentDidUpdate() {
  Perf.stop()
  Perf.printOperations()
}
```

Running the component, clicking +, and checking the console should give us all the answers.

What we can see is that React, instead of inserting the new element on top, swaps the text of the two existing elements and inserts the last item at the bottom as if it was new. The reason it does that is because we are using the index of the map function as the key.

In fact, the index always starts from 0 even if we push a new item to the top of the list so React thinks that we changed the values of the existing two and that we added a new element at index 2. The behavior is the same as we would have without using the key prop at all.

This is a very common pattern because we may think that providing any key is always the best solution but it is not like that. The key has to be unique and stable, identifying one, and only one, item.

To solve the problem we can, for example, use the value of the item if we expect it not to be repeated within the list, or create a unique identifier.

Spreading props on DOM elements

There is a common practice that has recently been described as an anti-pattern by *Dan Abramov*; it also triggers a warning in the console when you do it in your React application.

It is a technique that is widely used in the community and I have personally seen it multiple times in real-world projects. We usually spread the properties to the elements to avoid writing every single one manually, as follows:

```
<Component {...props} />
```

This works very well and it gets transpiled into the following code by Babel:

```
React.createElement(Component, props);
```

However, when we spread props into a DOM element, we run the risk of adding unknown HTML attributes, which is a bad practice.

The problem is not related only to the spread operator; passing non-standard properties one by one leads to the same issues and warnings. Since the spread operator *hides* the single properties we are spreading, it makes even harder to figure out what we are passing to the element.

To see the warning in the console, a basic operation we can do is render the following component:

```
const Spread = () =>  <div foo="bar" />
```

The message we get looks like the following:

```
Unknown prop `foo` on <div> tag. Remove this prop from the element
```

Because the `foo` property is not valid for a `div` element.

In this case, as we said, it is easy to figure out which attribute we are passing and remove it but, if we use the spread operator, as in the following example:

```
const Spread = props => <div {...props} />
```

We cannot control which properties are passed from the parent.

If we use the component in this way:

```
<Spread className="foo" />
```

There are no issues.

But if we do something like:

```
<Spread foo="bar" className="baz" />
```

Then React complains because we are applying a non-standard attribute to the DOM element.

One solution we can use to solve the problem is to create a prop called **domProps** that we can spread safely to the component because we are explicitly saying that it contains valid DOM properties.

For example, we can change the `Spread` component in the following way:

```
const Spread = props => <div {...props.domProps} />
```

And use it in this way:

```
<Spread foo="bar" domProps={{ className: 'baz' }} />
```

As we have seen many times, with React it's always a good practice to be explicit.

Summary

Knowing all the best practices is always a good thing, but sometimes being aware of anti-patterns help us avoid taking the wrong path. Most importantly, learning the reasons why some techniques are considered bad practice helps us understand how React works and how we can use it effectively.

In this chapter, we covered four different ways of using components that can harm the performance and behavior of our web applications.

For each one of those, we used an example to reproduce the problem, and supplied the changes to apply in order to fix the issue.

We learned why using properties to initialize the state can result in inconsistencies between the state and the props, and we discovered why mutating the state is bad for performance. We also saw how using the wrong key attribute can produce bad effects on the reconciliation algorithm; and, finally, we learned why spreading non-standard props to DOM elements is considered an anti-pattern.

12
Next Steps

React is one of the most amazing libraries that have been released in the last years, not only because of the library itself and its great features but, most importantly, due to the ecosystem that has been built around it.

Following the React community is very exciting and inspiring: there are new projects and tools to learn and play with every single day. Not just that, there are conferences and meetups where you can talk to people in real life and build new relationships, blog posts that you can read to improve your skills and learn more, and many other ways to become a better developer.

React and its ecosystem are encouraging best practices and a love for open source in developers, which is fantastic for the future of our careers.

In this chapter, we will see the following:

- How to contribute to the React library by opening issues and Pull Requests
- Why it is important to give back to the community and share your code
- The most important aspects to keep in mind when pushing open source code
- How to publish an npm package and how to use semantic versioning

Contributing to React

One thing that people often want to do when they've used React for a while is to contribute to the library. React is open source which means that its source code is public and anyone who's signed the **Contributor License Agreement (CLA)** can help to fix bugs, write documentation, or even add new features.

You can read the full terms of the CLA at the following URL:

```
https://code.facebook.com/cla
```

Suppose, for example, you were building an application with React and you found a bug, what should you do? The first and most important thing is to create a small reproducible example of the problem. To do that, there is a handy **JSFiddle** template provided by the React team:

```
https://jsfiddle.net/reactjs/69z2wepo/
```

This operation has two key benefits:

- It helps you to be 100% confident that the bug is effectively a React bug and not just an issue with your application code
- It helps the React team understand the problem quickly without having to delve into your application code, making the process faster

The Fiddle uses the latest version of React and this is important because, if you find a bug in an older version of the library, it may already have been fixed in the current one. Vice versa; if you find a problem with the latest version of the library that was not in the previous versions, it is a regression and it is going to have a higher priority because it may affect a massive number of users.

Once the little demo to show the problem is ready, you can file an issue on GitHub:

```
https://github.com/facebook/react/issues/new
```

As you'll see, the issue comes with some pre-filled instructions, with one of those being to set up the minimal demo. The other questions help you to explain the problem and to describe current and the expected behaviors.

It is important for you to read the *Facebook Code of Conduct* before participating or contributing to the repository: `https://code.facebook.com/codeofconduct`. The document lists good behaviors that are expected from all community members and that everyone should follow.

Once the issue is filed, you have to wait for one of the core contributors to examine it and tell you what they've decided to do with the bug. Depending on the severity of it, they might fix it or ask you to fix it.

In the second case, you can fork the repository and write code to solve the problem. It is important to follow the coding style guides and write all the tests for the fix. It is also crucial that all the old tests pass to make sure the new code does not introduce regressions in the codebase.

When the fix is ready and all the tests are green, you can submit a **Pull Request** and wait for the core team members to review it. They may decide to merge it or ask you to make some changes.

If you did not find a bug but you still want to contribute to the project you can look into the issues tagged with the **good first bug** label on GitHub:

```
https://github.com/facebook/react/labels/good%20first%20bug
```

This is a great way to start contributing and it is fantastic that the React team gives everyone, especially new contributors, the possibility of being part of the project.

If you find a good first bug issue that has not been already taken by someone, you can add a comment on the issue saying that you are interested in working on it. One of the core members will get in touch with you. Make sure to discuss your approach and the path you want to take with them before starting coding so that you do not have to rewrite the code multiple times.

Another way of improving React is by adding new features. It is important to say that the React team has a plan to follow and the main features are designed and decided by the core members.

If you are interested in knowing what are the next steps the library will take, you can find some of them under the label **big picture** on GitHub:

```
https://github.com/facebook/react/issues?q=is:open+is:issue+label:%22big+pict
ure%22
```

That said, if you have some good ideas about features that should be added to the library, the first thing to do is to open an issue and start talking with the React team. You should avoid spending time writing code and submitting a Pull Request before asking them because the feature you have in mind might not fit into their plans or might conflict with other functionalities they are working on.

Distributing your code

Contributing to the React ecosystem does not only mean pushing code into the React repository. To give back to the community and help developers, you can create packages, blog posts, answer questions on Stack Overflow, and many other activities.

Suppose for example you created a React component that solves a complex problem and you think that other developers would benefit from using it instead of investing time in building their solutions. The best thing to do is to publish it to GitHub and make it available for everyone to read and use. However, pushing the code to GitHub is only a small action within a big process and it comes with some responsibilities. So you should have a clear idea in mind about the reasons behind your choice.

One of the motivations why you may want to contributes to improve your skills as a developer. Sharing your code, in fact, on the one hand forces you to follow best practice and write better code. On the other hand, it exposes your code to feedback and comments from other developers. This is a big opportunity for you to receive tips and improve your code to make it better.

Other than the suggestions related to the code itself, by pushing your code to GitHub you benefit from other people's ideas. In fact, you might have thought about a single problem that your component can solve but another developer may use it in a slightly different way, finding new solutions for it. Moreover, they might need new features and they could help you implement them so that everyone, yourself included, can benefit from it. Building software together is great to improve both your skills and your packages and that is why I strongly believe in open source.

Another significant opportunity that open source can give you is letting you get in touch with smart and passionate developers from all around the world. Working closely with new people who have different backgrounds and skill sets is one of the best ways to keep our minds open and improve ourselves.

Sharing code also gives you some responsibilities and it could be time-consuming. In fact, once the code is public and people can use it, you have to maintain it.

Maintaining a repository requires commitment because the more popular it gets and the more people use it, the higher the number of questions and issues will be. For example, developers may encounter bugs and open issues, so you have to go through all of them and try to reproduce the problems. If the problems exist, then you have to write the fix and publish a new version of the library. You could receive Pull Requests from developers, which could be long and complex, and they need to be reviewed.

If you decide to ask people to co-maintain the project and help you with issues and Pull Requests you have to coordinate with them to share your vision and make decisions together. With this in mind, we can go through some good practices which can help you make a better repository and avoid some of the common pitfalls.

First of all, if you want to publish your React component you have to write a comprehensive set of tests. With public code and many people contributing to it, tests are very helpful for many reasons:

- They make the code more robust
- They help other developers understand what the code does
- They make it easier to find regression when new code is added
- They make other contributors more confident in writing the code

The second important thing to do is add a README with description of the component, an example of its use, and documentations of the APIs and props that can be used.

This helps users of the package but it also avoids people opening issues and asking questions about how the library works and how it should be used.

It is also essential to add a LICENSE file to your repository in order to make people aware of what they can and cannot do with your code. GitHub has a lot of ready-made templates to choose from.

Whenever you can, you should keep the package small and add as few dependencies as you can. Developers tend to think carefully about size when they have to decide whether to use a library or not. Remember that heavy packages have a bad impact on performance.

Not only that, depending on too many third-party libraries can create problems if any of them are not maintained or have bugs.

One tricky part in sharing React components comes when you have to decide about the styling. Sharing JavaScript code is pretty straightforward, while attaching the CSS is not as easy as you may think. In fact, there are many different paths you can take to provide it: from adding a CSS file to the package to using inline styles. The important thing to keep in mind is that CSS are global and generic class names may conflict with the ones that already exist in the project where the component is imported.

The best choice is to include the fewest possible styles and make the component highly configurable for end users. In this way developers will be more likely to use it because it can be adapted to their custom solutions.

To show that your component is highly customizable you can add one or more examples to the repository to make it easy for everyone to understand how it works and which props it accepts. Examples are also useful for you to test new versions of the component and see if there are unexpected breaking changes.

As we saw in `Chapter 3`, *Create Truly Reusable Components*, tools such as **React Storybook** can help you create living style guides, which are easier for you to maintain and for the consumer of your package to navigate and use.

An excellent example of a highly customizable library that uses Storybook to show all the variations is `react-dates` from AirBnb. You should take that repository as the perfect example of how to publish React components to GitHub.

As you can see, they use Storybook to show the different options of the component:

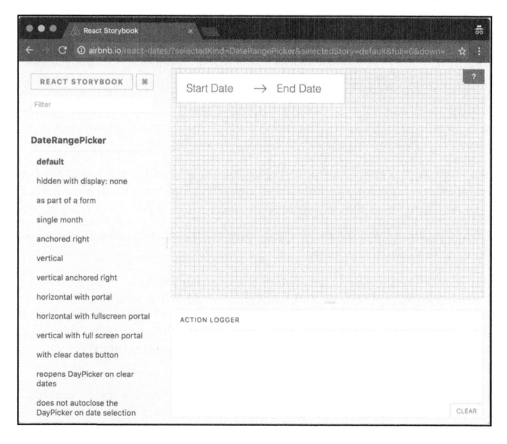

Last but not least, you not only want to share your code, but you may also want to distribute your package. The most popular package manager for JavaScript is npm, which we've used through the book to install packages and dependencies.

In the next section, we will see how easy is it to publish a new package with npm.

Other than npm, some developers may need to add your component as a global dependency and use it without a package manager.

As we saw in the first chapter, you can easily use React by just adding a script tag pointing to unpkg.com. It is important to give the users of your library the same option.

So, to offer a global version of your package, you should build the **Universal Module Definition (UMD)** version as well. With **Webpack** this is pretty straightforward: You just have to set the librarytarget in the output section of the configuration file.

Publishing a npm package

The most popular way of making a package available to developers is publishing it to npm, the package manager for Node.js.

We used it in all the examples in this book and you have seen how easy it is to install a package: It is just a matter of running npm install package, and that is it. What you may not know is how easy it is to publish a package as well.

First of all, if you move into an empty directory and write in your terminal:

```
npm init
```

A new package.json is created and some questions will be displayed. The first one is the package name, which defaults to the folder name, and then the version number. These are the most important ones because the first is the name that the users of your package will refer to when they install and use it; the second helps you release new versions of your package safely and without breaking other people's code.

The version number is composed of three numbers separated by a dot and they all have a meaning. The last number of the package on the right represents the patch, and it should be increased when a new version of the library that contains bug fixes is pushed to npm.

The number in the middle indicates the minor version of the release and it should be changed when new features are added to the library and those new features do not break existing APIs.

Finally, the first number on the left represent the major version and it has to be increased when a version containing breaking changes is released to the public.

Following this approach, called **Semantic Versioning (SemVer)**, is good practice and it makes your users more confident when they have to update your package.

The first version of a package is usually the 0.1.0.

To publish an npm package you must have an npm account, which you can easily create by running the following command in the console:

```
npm adduser $username
```

Where $username is the name of your choice.

Once the user is created you can run:

```
npm publish
```

A new entry will be added to the registry with the package name and the version you specified in the package.json.

Whenever you change something in your library and you want to push a new version, you just have to run:

```
npm version $type
```

Where $type is one patch, minor or major. This command will bump the version automatically in your package.json and it will also create a commit and a tag if your folder is under version control.

Once the version number is increased you just have to run npm publish again and the new version will be available to users.

Summary

In the last stop in this trip around the React world, we have seen some of the aspects that make React great: its community and its ecosystem, and how to contribute to them.

You learned how to open an Issue if you find a bug in React, and the steps to take to make it easier for its core developers to fix it. You now know the best practices when making code open source and the benefits and the responsibilities that come with it.

Finally, you saw how easy it is to publish packages on the npm registry and how to choose the right version number to avoid breaking other people's code.

Index

Printed in Great Britain
by Amazon

35282829R00181